D0616741

BOWLING GREEN STATE UNIVERSITY

DISCARDED

LIBRARY

The Demand for Energy
and Conservation in
the United States

**CONTEMPORARY STUDIES IN
ENERGY ANALYSIS AND POLICY, VOLUME 1**

Editor: Noel D. Uri, *Department of Economics and Business Administration, The Catholic University of America*

CONTEMPORARY STUDIES IN
ENERGY ANALYSIS AND POLICY
A Series of International Monographs, Texts and Treaties

Series Editor: Noel D. Uri
Department of Economics and Business Management
The Catholic University of America

Volume 1.   **THE DEMAND FOR ENERGY AND CONSERVATION IN THE UNITED STATES**
Noel D. Uri, *Department of Economic and Business Management, The Catholic University of America*

Volume 2.   **THE DYNAMIC DEMAND FOR ENERGY STOCKS: An Analysis of Tax Policy Options for Solar Processess**
G. Thomas Sav, *Department of Economics, West Georgia College*

Volume 3.   **SOLAR HOME HEATING AND CONSERVATION OPTIONS: An Economic Analysis**
Brent G. Kroetch, *Department of Economics, The American University*

Volume 4.   **ECONOMETRIC STUDIES OF ENERGY DEMAND AND SUPPLY**
Noel D. Uri, *Department of Economic and Business Management, The Catholic University of America*

JEROME LIBRARY–BOWLING GREEN STATE UNIVERSITY

To Ellen and Brian,
whose forecasts are probably
better than these

The Demand for Energy and Conservation in the United States

by NOEL D. URI
*Department of Economics and
Business Administration
Catholic University of America*

 **JAI PRESS INC.**

Greenwich, Conntecticut   *London, England*

Library of Congress Cataloging in Publication Data

Uri, Noel D.
  The demand for energy and conservation in the
United States.

  (Contemporary studies in energy analysis and
policy; v. 1)
  Includes index.
  1. Energy consumption—United States.
2. Energy conservation—United States.   I. Title.
II. Series.
HD9502.U52U738   1982   333.79′0973   82-81205
ISBN 0-89232-278-0   AACR2

Copyright © 1982 JAI PRESS INC.
36 Sherwood Place
Greenwich, Connecticut 06830

JAI PRESS INC.
3 Henrietta Street
London WC2E 8LU
England

All rights reserved. No part of this publication may be reproduced,
stored on a retrieval system, or transmitted in any form or by any
means, electronic, mechanical, filming, photocopying, recording or
otherwise without prior permission in writing from the publisher.

ISBN NUMBER: 0-89232-278-0
Library of Congress Catalog Card Number: 82-81205
Manufactured in the United States of America

CONTENTS

List of Figures		*xi*
List of Tables		*xiii*
Preface		*xv*

I. Introductory Remarks — **1**
Introduction — 1
Examining the Substitution Potential — 4
The Notion of Elasticity — 5
Theoretical Considerations — 6
Measurement Problems — 9
A Perspective — 14
   Short-term Energy Demand Models — 15
   Mid-term Energy Demand Models — 17
A Caveat — 20
Interfuel Substitution — 22
Outline of the Study — 24

II. The Residential Demand for Energy — **29**
Introduction — 29
A Model of Aggregate Energy Demand — 32
Fuel Share Expenditure Determination — 36
   Background — 36
   Estimation Procedure — 39
   Data — 40
   Empirical Results — 40
Testing for Model Stability — 47
Conclusion — 49

III. **The Industrial Demand for Energy**   **53**

Introduction   53
Factor Substitutability   56
    Introductory Comments   56
    Theoretical Foundations   57
    A Test for Directional Causality   58
    A Methodological Note   61
    Data   62
    Filtering   63
    Directional Causality and the Demand for
    the Factors of Production   65
    Implications of the Results   69
Energy Substitution   70
Interfuel Substitution   73
    Background   73
    A Price Possibility Frontier for
    Fuel Inputs   74
    Estimation Procedure   78
    Data   79
    Empirical Results   79
    Policy Implications   85
Testing for Model Stability   86
Conclusion   88

IV. **The Transportation Demand for Energy**   **93**

Introduction   93
Motor Gasoline Demand   95
    Background   95
    The Model Formulation   96
    Data   98
    Estimation Results   99
Diesel Fuel Demand   102
The Demand for Aviation Fuel   105
The Transportation Demand for Electrical Energy   106
Interfuel Substitution   107
    Background   107
    Estimation Procedure   111
    Data   112
    Empirical Results   112
Testing for Model Stability   117
Conclusions   119

V.   **The Demand for Energy By Electric Utilities**   **123**
    Introduction   123
    Theoretical Background   126
    Aggregate Energy Inputs   127
    Fuel Share Determination   131
      Background   131
      Estimation Procedure   133
      Data   134
      Empirical Results   134
    Testing for Model Stability   141
    Conclusions   143

VI.   **An Overview of the Energy Demand Analysis System**   **147**
    Introduction   147
    Structure of the System   147
    The Equation Specifications   150
    Some Reflective Caveats   154
      Uncertainty   154
      Simplifying Assumptions   155
    Conclusions   157

VII.   **Forecasting the Demand for Energy**   **159**
    Introduction   159
    Performance   159
    Assumptions   162
    Orientation   164
    Scenario Discussion   166
    General Forecast Results   170
      Base Case   170
      Slow Economic Growth   173
      Rising World Crude Oil Price   173
    Sector Energy Demand   174
      Residential Sector   174
      Industrial Sector   175
      Transportation Sector   177
      Electric Utility Sector   178
    Conclusions   179

VIII.   **Conclusions**   **183**
    Introduction   183
    General Conclusions   185
    Consummatory Remarks   187

Index   **189**

List of Figures

Chapter VI

1. Energy Demand Analysis System   148

List of Tables

Chapter I

1. Energy Expenditures Shares, 1978   23

Chapter II

1. Residential Energy Use, 1978   31
2. Aggregate Energy Consumption for the Residential
    Sector   35
3. Parameter Estimates for the Translog Fuel
    Expenditure Shares Model   42
4. Regional Elasticities of Substitution for the Period
    1957–1978   43
5. Regional Price Elasticities of Demand for the Period
    1957–1978   44
6. Computed Value of the Stability Test Statistic ω   48

Chapter III

1. Energy Consumption in the Industrial Sector, 1978   55
2. Data Filters   64
3. Summary of the Regressions of Own Price on
    Quantity   66
4A. Summary of the Regressions of Price on
    Quantity   67
4B. Summary of the Regressions of Price of Labor on
    Quantity   67
4C. Summary of the Regressions of Price of Energy on
    Quantity   68
4D. Summary of the Regressions of Price of Materials
    on Quantity   68
5. Aggregate Energy Demand for the Industrial Sector   72
6. Parameter Estimates for the Translog Energy Models   81

7. Estimates of Two-Digit Industry Price Elasticities,
   1958–1978   82
8. Computed Value of the Test Statistic ω   88

Chapter IV

1. Energy Consumption in the Transportation Sector   94
2. Stock of Automobiles   100
3. Utilization Rate of Automobiles   100
4. Diesel Fuel Demand   104
5. Aviation Fuel Demand   106
6. Electrical Energy Transportation Demand   108
7. Parameter Estimates for the Translog Energy
   Expenditures Shares Model   114
8. Elasticities of Demand for the Transportation Sector   115
9. Computed Value of the Stability Test Statistic ω   118

Chapter V

1. Electrical Energy End Use Consumption and Fuel
   Consumption for 1978 (in Percent)   124
2. Aggregate Energy Input for Electrical Energy
   Generation   129
3. Parameter Estimates for the Translog Fuel Model   136
4. Regional Elasticities of Substitution for the Period
   1961–1978   137
5. Regional Price Elasticities of Demand for the Period
   1961–1978   138
6. Computed Value of the Stability Test
   Statistic ω   143

Chapter VI

1. Generation of Electrical Energy   153

Chapter VII

1. Forecasting Errors for United States Energy Demand,
   1965–1980   161
2. Summary of Forecasts (in Percent)   171
3. Summary of Residential Forecasts (in Percent)   174
4. Summary of Industrial Forecasts (in Percent)   176
5. Summary of Transportation Forecasts (in Percent)   177
6. Summary of Electric Utility Forecasts (in Percent)   178

Preface

The fact that the level of gross national product (GNP) is closely related to the level of energy consumption has long been observed. A number of studies have established a relationship between per capita GNP and per capita energy consumption. The strategic role of energy can be appreciated if one thinks of energy as a factor of production. In contemporary economic thought, there are three basic factors of production: land, labor, and capital. Given a certain technological environment, energy can either be considered a fourth factor of production or, alternatively, as a complement to all productive processes which require the use of capital. In the analysis at hand energy is treated as a separate factor.

Productivity differentials between industries can partially be explained in terms of resource and equipment differences. Quantitative attempts to explain the origins of interindustry differences in production often put energy in place of capital. Energy is described as an index of a certain kind of capital, namely energy-consuming capital of all types. Both energy consumption and capital consumption measure in different ways the productive apparatus of the economy. Studies conducted in both the United States and the United Kingdom show a high correlation between energy consumption and the level of capital stock.

Energy is intrinsically an essential economic factor. Although there is indeed no immediate substitute for energy, in the longer run a given energy source can sometimes be substituted for by varying the factors of production. For example, there exists the possibility of interchange among individual fuels. Some uses are not interchangeable (e.g., the use of natural gas as a feedstock to produce ammonia), but for many other activities it matters little to industrial or residential consumers whether they obtain power and heat from coal, oil, natural gas, or electrical energy generated by one of these primary fuels. Rather, the choice among the various sources of energy is dependent on such things as price, cost of equipment, and convenience in usage.

Over the longer term, it is quite likely that interfuel substitution will increase because the consumption of electrical energy is growing at a faster rate than total energy consumption and it is in the electrical energy sector that the different fuels are most substitutable. Many generating plants have multifuel capabilities giving them a wide freedom of choice. Large consumers are therefore willing and able to shift from one fuel to another. The primary factor that influences the consumer is the price.

It is these issues of factor substitutability and interfuel substitution that are the focus of the following analysis. They offer considerable hope that the energy concerns characteristic of the past decade for the United States may in time be mitigated.

Finally, I would like to thank the Catholic University of America for providing me with a pleasant environment in which to conduct this research.

Noel D. Uri

Chapter I

Introductory Remarks

INTRODUCTION

Until the events of the decade of the 1970s, the expectations were that the demand for energy in the United States would continue its historical growth of 3.4 percent per year. Prior to 1970, abundant supplies of energy at relatively low prices existed. Markets for new energy-using technologies (e.g., air conditioning) were expanding rapidly, and the growth in energy demand coincided with the growth in the level of economic activity. During the two decades prior to 1970, gross national product (GNP)—in real terms—grew at an annual rate of 3.2 percent. Moreover, the year-to-year fluctuations in both aggregate energy demand and GNP were highly correlated.[1] This observation led to the conclusion that continued growth in energy consumption was inexorably intertwined with growth in the economy.[2]

The historical period witnessed a significant change in the composition of final energy demand in the form of interfuel substitution. In essence, this substitution is the story of the progressive erosion of the importance of coal as the dominant energy resource. Fuel oil in the decades of the 1920s and 1930s invaded coal's heating market. Diesel oil in the years after World War II effectively eliminated the railroad market for coal and severely eroded its marine transportation market. Congruently, natural gas combined with fuel oil to eradicate coal from the residential heating market while mitigating the importance of oil in that market.

1

The competition between fossil fuels was intense. By the early 1950s the energy profile observed today had emerged. Oil (liquid petroleum) is the preferred energy source in the transportation sector, whereas oil and natural gas share the heating market in the residential sector. The remaining important market for coal (besides the use for coke manufacture in the production of steel) is the utility boiler fuel market in which it competes with other energy sources.

In addition to the competition among fossil fuels (although this competition has been distorted because of the artificial maintenance of price differentials through regulation)[3] there is the competition between fossil fuels, on the one hand, and electrical energy, on the other. This competition between the fuels and electrical energy has existed since the inception of the electric power industry. Electric lighting replaced natural gas and oil lamps. Moreover, as the twentieth century progressed, electrical energy could be used to power a larger variety of energy-using appliances and equipment. In 1978, for example, electrical energy accounted for about one-fourth of all primary energy consumed.

By 1970, the energy system began to significantly alter its structure. The regulation of the price of natural gas became an increasingly controversial issue, and the initial curtailments of natural gas consumption occurred in order to allocate the limited supply (at prevailing regulated prices) in the face of increasing demand. Domestic production of crude oil began to decline.

The environmental issues associated with burning fossil fuels was of national concern. The regulation of emissions from generating plants, for example, was hotly debated.[4] Further, the Organization of Petroleum Exporting Countries (OPEC) oil embargo and precipitous price increases created new concerns for the U.S. economy.

The resultant new awareness of the critical role of energy has led to a careful examination of the importance of energy in the U.S. economy as well as forecasts of the probable demand for energy for the rest of the century. At one extreme, there is the view that the consumption of energy will rise in a fixed proportion to the level of the economy. From this point of view, which de facto is supported by energy and GNP data for the United States prior to 1970, economic growth determines energy demand. Energy demand, therefore, has to be treated as a requirement to be met to facilitate the desired level of economic expansion. At the other extreme, the view exists that the increased consumption of energy is only one of a myriad of ways to approach the desired objectives and the quantity demanded can be reduced without imposing significant penalties, thus conserving resources for future generations in addition to maintaining environmental quality.[5]

The actual situation undoubtedly lies somewhere between the two polar cases. The evaluation of the potential flexibility of energy consumption (through, e.g., interfuel substitution) will have a large impact on the types of policies recommended. Those who perceive energy demand as being inflexible favor programs to expand energy supply. The argument typically runs that even with a finite resource base of fossil fuels, only a fraction is economically recoverable. Through higher prices (via deregulation), the economically recoverable resource base can be expanded despite the fixity of the total resource base. Moreover, other energy forms, such as solar and fusion, offer unlimited energy reserves.[6]

Those who view energy as being substitutable (e.g., S.D. Freeman), suggest that there are many wasteful uses of energy that with appropriate incentives (e.g., tax credits, legislatively mandated low thermostats, automobile fuel efficiency standards) can be eliminated.[7]

The purpose of what follows is to critically assess the feasibility of energy conservation through price-induced effects and to a limited extent non-price-related measures. No effort is made to evaluate the complexities of the economics of energy supply. This is properly the topic of another endeavor. In the final analysis, no prescription can be proferred as to the ideal combination of conservation incentives and production stimulations. By quantifying the magnitude of the potential for energy conservation, however, some demonstration can be made as to the gap that must be filled by increased energy production.

To effectively determine the potential for energy conservation, an analysis of the determinants of aggregate energy demand and specific energy sources is needed. More precisely, the energy substitution potential must be delineated—that is, between energy and nonenergy factors and among individual energy sources. Substitution between energy and other factors of production are important in assessing the extent to which the growth in the level of economic activity is independent of the availability of energy. If the possibility exists for substituting capital, labor, and/or materials in the industrial sector for energy, then the supposedly fixed energy–GNP relationship can be varied.

Of equal importance is the possibility of substituting one energy source (e.g., coal) for another (e.g., electrical energy). As briefly noted, there is a history of coal having been replaced by alternative energy forms in the United States. Differing availabilities and technical qualities of the various energy sources necessitates conservation policy that focuses on reducing the consumption of some types of energy more than others. Furthermore, the long-run supply potential between energy types is different. The abundant reserves of coal in the United States (currently estimated to be 475 billion tons, or enough to last for 672 years at the current rate of consumption)[8] are in marked relief to estimates of crude oil and natural gas reserves.[9]

Given the various technological characteristics and long-run availabilities of energy types, conservation policies should focus on specific energy types with the achievement of aggregate energy conservation the result of reducing the consumption of specific forms of energy. This approach opens up new substitution possibilities not available if individual energy source conservation is realized only by aggregate energy conservation. By recognizing the difference in availabilities the way is clear to substitute relatively less expensive for more expensive energy types.

EXAMINING THE SUBSTITUTION POTENTIAL

The beginning point in the analysis of the demand for energy is to treat energy as an economic good. In particular, energy is only one factor used in the manufacturing process or the household production process.[10] This approach is motivated by the possibility of trade-offs between energy and other goods.

The profit-maximizing firm and the cost-minimizing consumer will consider the prices of all inputs when making decisions about the configuration of goods and services to be used. As the price of energy rises relative to other factors, economic agents will take advantage of the opportunities to substitute more energy-efficient machinery, to improve the thermal integrity of buildings, to switch to alternate modes of transportation, etc. The energy consumer makes these and many other substitutions in order to minimize the cost of meeting the fundamental objective of producing a given level of output or reaching a given level of satisfaction (utility).

The magnitude of these adjustments is dependent upon such things as technical feasibility and subjective preferences. The measurement of the energy substitution potential, in order to adequately reflect these factors, has to be based on observed behavior of energy consumers who are confronted with differential prices as well as the possibility of making energy choices. The effect (although not the precise sequence) will be reported by a reduction in the quantity of energy demanded in percentage terms, ceteris paribus in response to a given percentage increase in price. The ratio is the elasticity of energy demand. Since the notion of elasticity is critical to what follows, it is useful to examine it in more detail.

THE NOTION OF ELASTICITY

The notion of elasticity of demand was first introduced by Alfred Marshall in the *Principles of Economics*.[11] He suggests that "the elasticity of demand in a market is great or small according to how the amount demanded increases much or little for a given fall in price, and diminishes much or little for a given rise in price" (p. 102). More precisely, the elasticity of demand is defined as the percent change in quantity demanded for a specific good or service given a 1 percent change in price, all other factors remaining unchanged. At its inception, the elasticity notion met with considerable applause.[12]

The domain in which the analysis of demand was introduced was one of partial equilibrium analysis, that is, studying a specific sector as an element of a more comprehensive system. By making the concession that the elasticity of demand is computed holding all other elements constant at a given level, it is natural to also express the elasticity of demand for a good or service with respect to variations in the price of any other commodity (cross-price elasticity), with respect to variations in the prices of all commodities (factors as well as products), and with respect to variations in income.[13] In this instance, elasticity concepts become tools of general analysis to be used for the purpose of exploring relations in which we are primarily interested because they also assert themselves in the economy as a whole.

Despite the utility of the elasticity concept in empirical studies there has been less than unanimity in agreeing to its overall usefulness. Thus, for example, Paul A. Samuelson suggests that the importance of elasticity coefficients "is not very great except possibly as mental exercise for beginning students."[14] His reason for this observation is that most of the laws of economics are qualitative and ordinal (e.g., the Law of Demand) rather than quantitative and, where this is the case, the problem of dimension is of no consequence. Moreover, while elasticity expressions are invariant under changes of scale, they are not invariant under changes of origin. Since there are no natural zeros from which one can measure economic magnitudes, the elasticity expressions are essentially arbitrary. Thus, when such items as imports of crude oil and amount of factors supplied are encountered, all are measured from an arbitrary base.[15]

Ultimately the acceptance or rejection of the use of the elasticity concept rests on a subjective basis. If we are willing to overlook some valid theoretical objections in favor of the utilitarianism of the elasticity concept, then the concept is potentially useful in helping us gain insight into energy concerns.

THEORETICAL CONSIDERATIONS

The objective in the estimation of demand relations is to determine the social value of energy products as revealed in market activity. The basic relationships underlying social value are individual preference functions and their cumulation into aggregates. It is typically assumed that aggregate (i.e., society's) preferences can be represented by a well-behaved preference function of the final goods and services consumed. Additionally, it is assumed that the economic agents (both consumers and producers) act, in the long-run, to attain the most preferred set of goods and services. It is important to note that consumers in this setting desire energy services (e.g., space heating and cooling) while energy products (e.g., electrical energy and natural gas) are only a means to fulfilling these desires.

Consumers are confronted with a budget constraint of the form

$$M = P^e \cdot E + X, \tag{1.1}$$

where M denotes money income;

P^e is a vector of dimension n denoting the relative prices of energy services to nonenergy goods;

E is a vector of dimension n denoting the quantity of energy services consumed; and

X is the quantity of nonenergy goods and services consumed.

The preference function is not directly observable but ostensibly can be reconstructed from observed data (i.e., revealed preference). This is done simply by observing how consumers respond to different prices and incomes. Each time a consumer is confronted with a price–income combination (P^e, M) a choice of (E, X) is made. Observation of a series of such combinations and choices can be used to construct a preference function.

De facto, when trying to implement this sort of technique, a sufficient number of observations are seldom available to make it viable. In addition, the presumption that tastes remain static over the period of observation is frequently violated, as are the other ceteris paribus assumptions (price of other goods and services constant, money income constant, etc.). An approximation of the preference function can be made by specifying an exact functional form and estimating econometrically the coefficients of this function.

There are a myriad of possible exact preference functional forms. For illustrative purposes, one that is separable over time (suggested by Nordhaus)[16] is used here. If S_t is an index of consumption and taking nonenergy goods as the *numéraire*, the preference function is

$$S_t = X_t + \sum_{i=1}^{n} \theta_i E_{it}^{-\alpha_i}(X_t + \sum_{i=1}^{n} \phi_i E_{it})^{\beta_i}, \qquad (1.2)$$

where X_t denotes an index of nonenergy goods in period t;

E_{it} denotes different energy services (i = 1, 2, . . . , n) in period t; and

θ_i, α_i, and β_i denote parameters of the preference function.

The ϕ_i values are taken to be the base period weights for energy in terms of other (nonenergy) goods so that the term in parenthesis is M_t.

Maximizing Eq. (1.2) subject to the budget constraint given in Eq. (1.1) (that is, $\Sigma\ P_{it}^e E_{it} + X_t = M_t$, where P_{it}^e are the current year prices of specific energy services relative to an index of nonenergy prices) yields the following energy demand functions:

$$E_{it} = \zeta_i(P_{it}^e)^{-\gamma_i}(M_t)^{\delta_i} \qquad (i = 1, 2, \ldots, n), \qquad (1.3)$$

where $\zeta_i = (\alpha_i \theta_i)^{1/(1-\alpha_i)}$;

$\gamma_i = 1/(1 - \alpha_i)$;   and

$\delta_i = \beta_i/(1 - \alpha_i)$.

Observe that all of the coefficients in the original preference function are identified although there is no guarantee of uniqueness (because of the nonlinearity).

Typically, in Eq. (1.2) we would expect $0 < \alpha_i < 1$ and $0 < \beta_i < 1$ so that the demand for energy services is inversely related to price and directly related to income.

Moreover, this approach presents a specific basis on which to estimate energy demand elasticities. In this instance the demand elasticity, d log E_{it}/d log P_{it}, is simply γ_i.

This, then, using contemporary neoclassical microeconomic theory, is the theoretical justification for and approach to estimating demand and elasticities of demand. There is nothing theurgic about the form of the preference function used beyond its being flexible enough to determine the more important properties of a general preference function. Considerable literature on the precise configuration of this preference function exists (see Arrow[17] for a nice survey of this). More elaborate treatments introduce additional factors into the final form of the energy demand equations, but all—in combination with the budget constraint [i.e., Eq. (1.1)—do give demand functions.

The obvious question, with a view toward estimating *the* demand equation, concerns the precise configuration and appropriate exact functional representation of the preference function. As alluded to earlier, we do not know what these preference functions look like so it is impossible to know the one exact functional form for the demand equation that yields an exact, quantitative estimate of demand elasticities.

Where does this leave the estimation of demand elasticities? The investigation into this question is the topic of the next section.[18]

MEASUREMENT PROBLEMS[19]

Studies of demand have involved the three basic objectives of econometrics: structural analysis, forecasting, and policy evaluation. Two seminal studies, those by Wold and Jureen[20] and Stone,[21] illustrate all three uses of empirical studies of demand; moreover, they extensively treat the important measurement issues in estimating demand relationships, namely, the questions of functional form, identification, aggregation, and dynamic considerations. As a result of looking at these, it becomes clear that there is no single ideal model for empirical research on demand. Rather, it is necessary to structure the model around the particular phenomenon under investigation. A cursory examination of these issues should make this abundantly clear.

Before doing this, however, it is necessary to reiterate that the application of econometrics to the theory of demand requires, in addition to the data, a specific formal econometric model. The demand for any good in general (the example of the foregoing section excepted) is a function of the price of the good itself, of income, and of the price of all other goods and services.

Econometric studies of demand include both single demand equations and studies of systems of demand equations. A single demand equation study selects one equation and estimates its parameters (e.g., the price coefficient). An econometric study of the system of demand equations estimates the complete system for a group of consumers. A priori, on theoretical grounds, the demand system should be selected.[22] On practical grounds it is frequently impossible to estimate a system so that single-equation models must be resorted to even though they only approximately satisfy the constraints imposed by static neoclassical microeconomic theory.

It is now appropriate to turn to examination of some of the measurement issues:

1. Functional form. The program in choosing the functional form is that good formal sequential testing procedures remain to be developed (see Zellner[23]). Tests do exist (see Ramsey[24]) for the appropriate functional form, but serious questions have been raised as to the power of such tests (see Taylor[25]). Thus, for single-equation models, the choice of a linear form, semilogarithmic form, linear-in-logarithms (double-logarithmic form), or some nonlinear form is usually based on such factors as goodness of fit in addition to ease of estimation and immediacy of interpretation (see Houthakker[26]).

In the case of systems of demand equations, the choice is generally restricted to linear, linear-in-logarithms, and linear expenditure systems. In the case of the linear expenditure system (developed by Stone[27]), it is interpreted as stating that expenditure on a good can be decomposed into two components. The first is the expenditure on a certain base amount which is the minimum expenditure to which the consumer is committed. The second is a fraction of the so-called supernumerary income, defined as the income above the "subsistence income" needed to purchase base amounts of all goods. Once again, there is no theurgic way to choose one specification over another.

2. Identification. An important question in estimating demand relationships is that of identification: Has the demand equation been identified and, in particular, can it be distinguished from the supply equation? (See, e.g., Fisher.[28]) For example, assume a simultaneous system is specified whereby *demand* is a simple linear function of a constant term and price and *supply* is a simple linear function of a constant term and price. This system is, in general, not identified since when one only possesses information on price–quantity pairs it is not clear de facto whether one is observing the demand or the supply curves. The problem is not alleviated by adding more data points. Estimating the relationship by any number of data points would not provide enough information upon which to estimate the values of the four parameters.

One of two approaches is typically adopted in overcoming the identification problem. The first is based on the use of zero restrictions. This entails adding relevant variables to certain equations but not to others in order to differentiate the demand question from the supply equation and then to estimate each. For example, in the two-equation demand and supply framework alluded to previously, with the addition of an economic activity variable to the demand equation and rainfall to the supply equation, the identification problem is overcome because at least one of the factors causing each of the curves to shift has been explicitly included in the model. The second and less widely accepted approach to identification rests on the relative variances. In the context of a two-equation demand and supply system, if the variance of the stochastic term for the demand equation is significantly smaller than the corresponding variance of the supply equation, then a line through the observed price–quality combinations yields an approximation to the demand curve.

3. *Aggregation.* The basic theory of demand refers to a single consuming unit. Empirical work, however, usually involves market phenomena such as the total quantity purchased in a region. The problem of aggregation is that of reconciling the two.

A simple example of the aggregation problem and conditions of aggregation is that of the linear demand equation. Consider only own price and income as explanatory variables for an individual economic agent. Summing over all agents is a straightforward process. The term that presents a problem in this aggregation is that involving income since, in general, the marginal propensity to consume of the specific good varies from one agent to another. The aggregation condition for this problem comes down to assuming that the response of demand to income is the same for all agents. Generally, aggregation conditions must be imposed in order to develop aggregate demand equations from individual ones. Such conditions usually require that if an explanatory variable changes among different micro units (e.g., income) but the coefficients are the same for each such unit, then the macro relationship is of the same form where the explanatory variable is the sum of the micro variables. Additionally, they require that if an explanatory variable is the same for all of the micro units (e.g., price), then the macro relationship is of the same form but the coefficient in the macro relationship is the sum of the coefficients for the micro relationships.

An important practical implication of the problem of aggregation involves the type of data utilized and the nature of the hypotheses being examined. To the extent that the data being used in an empirical investigation are aggregates, such data typically are constructed on the basis of certain, usually implicit, assumptions. These assumptions are illustrated by the above conditions of aggregation. It is then inappropriate to test for these conditions, which would be tantamount to testing a maintained hypothesis.

4. Dynamic demand analysis. The theoretical constructs on which demand analysis was presented in the foregoing section rests on a static basis—a situation in which time plays no essential role. Note in passing, however, that a dynamic theory convenient for econometric functions has yet to be developed.

Dynamic elements need to be introduced into the preference function. The utility of energy-consuming durable goods, for example, is related to quantities purchased in a previous period. The difficulties, however, can be mitigated by assuming that preference functions arise from the quantity held (i.e., a stock concept). This, of course, leads to the problem of relating the level of purchases in any one period to the stocks held. Taking into account the effect of habit, we might assume that the preference function is influenced by previous purchases (e.g., an electric water heater), which will thus influence present purchases (e.g., electrical energy). We cannot assume that the income constraint will remain unchanged in a truly dynamic theory. In this setting, a consumer will avail himself of the possibilities of borrowing. This leads naturally to a concept of permanent income. A combination of the theory of the savings decision and the allocation decision is needed. This leaves, however, the purchases of durable commodities unexplained. Since durable goods are thought of as assets, a theory of portfolio decisions for the consumer is desirable. Unfortunately, this is not yet available; and even if it were, durables would present further difficulties since in many cases facilities for borrowing are specifically tied to durable items.

An additional complication that a truly dynamic theory might have to deal with is the *speculative effect:* If a consumer anticipates a price rise, he may speed up his purchase of a commodity.

Typically, empirical studies of dynamic demand reflect these difficulties by incorporation of ad hoc devices into the demand function. Perhaps the most straightforward of the dynamic specifications is that of a time trend in the demand equation. Inclusion of a variable to reflect the regular, constant shifting of the demand function over time is a straightforward and simple process. A second approach involves lagged variables. An example is a monthly model where the quantity demanded of electrical energy depends on lagged price, that is, the price of a previous period. This arises because of the institutional consideration of the consumer and not knowing at the time of consumption precisely what the price is because of the inclusion of, among other things, a fuel adjustment charge which varies monthly. (Elsewhere, Uri[29] explores this more fully.)

A third approach to modeling dynamic demand is the specification of a distributed lag relationship. Such a relationship is frequently utilized in studying the demand for consumer durables (e.g., energy-using capital equipment). The analysis is based on a partial adjustment model whereby the change in the variable of concern is proportional to the gap between the current desired magnitude and the past actual level. [A variant of this approach deals with the use of some form of the partial adjustment model, given some type of transformation (e.g., first differences, logarithmic) of the variable (e.g., demand) of interest.]

The final approach (the final one considered here) in looking at dynamic demand analysis is that of Houthakker and Taylor.[30] It is based on the idea that consumption involves some aspect of habit formation or inertia as individual consumers become accustomed to certain amounts of a good. This habit formation can be accounted for by an observable stock of goods in the case of habit-forming durables. The line of reasoning is extended to all goods and services. In the case of nondurables, e.g., specific forms of energy, the stock is unobservable and is essentially a psychological construct.

With the foregoing considerations, what are the general points that emerge with regard to the estimation of demand functions and demand elasticities? Simple methods for estimating demand relations are applicable only in specific cases. In general the determination of demand elasticities call for a full simultaneous model that is carefully designed to meet the specific conditions of the market under investigation. Further, the introduction of dynamic consideration is at best an ad hoc procedure.

These are the problems that have confronted energy researchers as they have endeavored to get a handle on the nature and extent of the responsiveness of the quantity of energy demanded to energy price changes.

A PERSPECTIVE

Before proceeding with the approach to demand modeling to be used in this study, it is useful to delve into energy demand research in more than just a cursory fashion to obtain an appreciation of what has heretofore been done. But because the field is so extensive, it is necessary to limit the examination of it. To this end, the models (both short term and mid term) used by the Office of Applied Analysis of the Energy Information Administration in the *Annual Report to Congress—1979* are examined.[31]

The philosophies underlying demand modeling in the short

term (on a quarterly basis for two years) and in the mid term (through 1995) are different and rest primarily on data availability. In the short term the focus is on final demand aggregated across all consuming sectors, whereas in the mid term the focus is on sectoral demand. (The sectors are residential, commercial, industrial, and transportation.) Neither of the approaches concerns itself with the problem of simultaneous equation bias (see measurement problem 2 in the previous section). All of the estimation is essentially based on single-equation models.

The approach now will be to discuss some of the demand models and their derived price elasticities with the realization that the approaches used in modeling the various components of total energy demand are those typically employed by researchers. It is up to the reader to decide whether the methodologies are proper (or at least acceptable) in light of our foregoing discussion concerning the theoretical foundation of demand analysis together with the inherent measurement problems.

The following analysis logically divides into two parts—focusing first on the short-term models and then on the mid-term models.

Short-term Energy Demand Models

Because of the dearth of high-frequency (monthly or quarterly) sectoral data, there is a long history of modeling short-term energy demand on an aggregate basis. Beginning with the report entitled *National Petroleum Product Supply and Demand 1975*,[32] the Office of Applied Analysis and its predecessors have looked almost exclusively at aggregate end use consumption (the exceptions being the sectoral models developed for natural gas and electrical energy; these have subsequently been relegated to the archives).

With regard to the demand for various refined petroleum products, the specifications of the demand for distillate fuel oil and the demand for residual fuel oil are simple linear equations where the monthly quantity demanded is a function of the own price of the fuel, weather (heating degree days), disposable personal income, seasonal (qualitative) factors, and a constant term. No provision for the dynamic adjustment process is made. The precise specification was decided upon based on a goodness-of-fit test. The price elasticity of demand for distillate fuel oil is estimated to be -0.12 (t statistic = 3.61). For residual fuel oil it is -0.70 (t statistic = 2.50). No cross-price elasticities are estimated.

The demand for motor gasoline was computed based on the definitional relationship demand being equal to vehicle miles traveled times the automobile stock divided by fleet efficiency. The critical component in this specification is the vehicle miles traveled (or use) computation. Use on a monthly basis is made a function of price, disposable personal income, and use in the previous period (month). The data were deseasonalized, so no seasonal factors are explicitly incorporated. The equation (aggregated for the entire United States) is specified in double-logarithmic form. Because of estimation problems, a survey of previous motor gasoline demand studies was used to reach a consensus on the price elasticity. An average value of -0.15 was decided upon. (Note that the short-term models are mainly used in a forecasting setting. Thus, the apparent arbitrariness in the selection of a price elasticity is not as problematic as it might appear.)

The demand for electrical energy is estimated in essentially the same way as the demand for distillate fuel oil and residual fuel oil. The monthly quantity demanded for the aggregate United States is a function of the price of electrical energy, economic activity, weather, and seasonal factors. The one departure is that the functional specification is semilogarithmic with the left-hand side (i.e., total demand) appropriately transformed. Interfuel substitution possibilities are not reflected (e.g., natural gas price is omitted) since they did not prove to be statistically significant for short-term considerations. The estimated monthly price elasticity of demand is -0.05 (t statistic = 1.96).

For the other components of refined petroleum products (e.g., jet fuel, propane, petrochemical feedstocks, and kerosene) and for natural gas and coal, explicit demand equations are not estimated. The reader interested in the methodology adopted is referred to reports on the Short-Term Integrated

Forecasting System (see, for example, that of the Short-Term Analysis Division[33]).

Now comes the difficult part. If one considers what has been done in the context of the foregoing discussion on the neo-classical theory underlying demand and the ever-present mea-surement problems, what can one conclude with regard to the meaning of the price elasticities? Unfortunately, not a great deal. It is clear that aggregating across fairly heterogeneous groups (sectors) of consumers imposes some heavy require-ments on the estimated coefficients. This problem is com-pounded when the aggregation across consuming regions is made. Additionally, the absence of explicit recognition of the dynamic element inherent in demand analysis only serves to confuse the issue more. The issue to be resolved is that, given a desire and (in some instances) requirement to make objective pronouncements concerning the responsiveness of the quantity of various types of energy demanded to changes in the price, but at the same time recognizing the need to have the analysis be consistent with accepted theory, can one find an acceptable formulation for short-term energy demand considerations?

Mid-term Energy Demand Models

There are four mid-term models that make up the Demand Analysis System: (1) a residential energy use model; (2) a com-mercial energy use model; (3) an industrial energy demand model; and (4) a transportation energy demand model. Since two of the four models are extensive engineering—economic structures and are fairly complex, no attempt will be made to provide a comprehensive summary of them. Our concern is with the demand for energy, so the observations will be limited to this area.

The Residential Sector.[34] The demand for energy for the residential sector does not start with an explicit representation of demand and derive the requisite (household) elasticities. Rather, it is suggested that consumers respond to changes in energy prices in three different ways and it is this response that is de facto represented. Thus, in the short-term, consumers change the way in which they utilize existing stocks of equipment. In the longer term, they also change the capital stocks by retrofit and by improving the efficiency of the capital stock. Consequently, the elasticity of demand is decomposed into three elements—energy usage, equipment fuel choice, and technical efficiency. The sum of these gives the aggregate elasticity of demand for a specific energy source.

To estimate household energy usage a double-logarithmic specification is used whereby the demand for energy is made a function of the prices of electrical energy, natural gas, and oil, per capital income, and two weather variables. The estimated usage elasticities (long term) average about − 1.50 (t statistic = 3.94). Cross-price elasticities are significant and possess the correct sign.

Equipment fuel choice was modeled using a logit specification such that the share of households using a given energy source is a function of energy prices, equipment prices per capital income, weather, proportion of households in urban areas, and proportion of households in single-family units. Consistently, the price elasticities are smaller than − 1.0 and statistically significant. Equipment choices do respond to energy price changes.

Calculation of the elasticities of technical efficiency with respect to the price of energy is purely subjective. They average about − 0.20 across types of appliances.

As noted, summation of the detailed elasticities produces estimates of aggregate elasticities. Unfortunately, the statistical basis for many of the elasticities (own price, cross price, and income) is weak. As an aside, in a forecasting setting the applicability of energy price elasticities derived from data from a period in which energy prices were declining to a future in which prices are likely to rise significantly is a problem of unknown dimension.

The Commercial Sector.[35]   The general structure (engineering–economic orientation) of the commercial demand for energy model bears a strong resemblance to the residential energy demand model. The actual computation of the demand for specific types of energy, however, is somewhat different. The modeling is done by building type for a specific type of energy and end use. Energy demand is specified to be a function of the stock of equipment (measured in terms of potential energy) and the utilization rate. The response of energy demand to price enters by making the utilization rate exclusively a function of the price of specific energy sources. Price elasticities were not estimated but rather adapted from a study by Baughman and Joskow.[36] The values used are -0.19 (t statistic = 1.99), -0.15 (t statistic = 4.01), -0.18 (t statistic = 3.66), and -0.15 (t statistic = 5.01) for electrical energy, natural gas, oil, and other fuels, respectively.

The Industrial Sector.[37]   The structure of the industrial demand model resembles the more traditional approach to demand modeling developed by Houthakker and Taylor.[38] Total demand per capita is made a function of price, economic activity (industrial production), weather, and demand in the previous period. Note that total demand is computed as a divisia index of the quantity of energy consumed. The model is linear in logarithms and is estimated by pooling cross-section and time series data. Elasticity estimates for the aggregate industrial sector (i.e., aggregation across specific industries) are -0.37 (t statistic = 6.21) for electrical energy, -0.39 (t statistic = 3.55) for natural gas, -0.53 (t statistic = 6.04) for distillate fuel oil, -0.45 (t statistic = 3.68) for residual fuel oil, and -0.35 (t statistic = 4.07) for coal. The cross-price elasticities generally have the correct sign but are very small in magnitude (on the order of 0.01 to 0.04).

The Transportation Sector.[39]   The demand for motor gasoline model in the mid-term resembles the short-term transportation energy demand structure. The demand for gasoline by automobiles is simply vehicle miles traveled (use) times vehicle stock divided by the average fleet fuel efficiency. Use is a function of population, personal income, the average workweek, and the price of gasoline. The fleet fuel efficiency is a function of the price of gasoline and the Environmental Protection Agency's *standardized efficiency factor.* Both equations are linear in logarithms. The estimated price elasticity when both the impact of price on use and its impact on fleet efficiency are taken into account is about -0.25 (no t statistic reported).

The demand for energy by trucks and buses is handled separately. Energy use by trucks is defined as being a function (linear in logarithm form) of the price of motor gasoline and distillate fuel oil, industrial production, and economic activity while the energy use by buses is a simple function of the prices of motor gasoline and distillate fuel oil and the level of economic activity. The elasticity of demand for the combined consumption of motor gasoline and distillate fuel oil is −0.55 (t statistic = 3.75) for trucks and −0.48 (t statistic = 4.50) for buses. The cross-price elasticity between distillate fuel oil and motor gasoline is about 0.30 (t statistic = 3.86).

The demand for energy by the other subcomponents of the transportation sector (e.g., air transportation and railroads) is estimated in a prosaic way. Using a double-logarithmic formulation, demand is characterized as a function of price, economic activity, and a factor to reflect historical trends. The estimated energy elasticity for air transportation (jet fuel) is −0.42 (t statistic = 2.09); for railroads, it is −0.62 (t statistic = 3.05). Cross-price elasticities are not estimated.

In the mid-term as in the short-term, specification and estimation of demand equations is more with an eye on expediency than with an eye on economic theory. As can be seen from the cursory foregoing discussion, many of the knotty problems are relegated entirely to the background. Is this acceptable? To be sure, the efforts in the mid-term area are more cognizant of the dynamic elements. One finds a discussion and incorporation of capital stock in the specifications (although in an ad hoc way) in two of the demand models. But what about the tendency to use the results of demand analysis (e.g., the quantity demanded is a function of price and income) without worrying about how and on what basis these results were derived? This question must be of concern in the following analysis.

A CAVEAT

The foregoing conclusions have focused on the general nature of demand analysis and the notion of the elasticity of demand. Specific examples were drawn from the models used by the Office of Applied Analysis of the Energy Information Administration in the U.S. Department of Energy. The same reservations expressed over these examples are applicable to almost all energy models. In the context of neoclassical microeconomic theory, do the models approximate closely enough the requisite conditions to give any substance to the belief that estimated elasticities are true reflections of the magnitude of the response of the quantity of energy demanded by consumers to variations in price? (Note that, although not discussed in detail, the same thought applies to the estimation of income elasticities.)

As an extention of the foregoing discussion, comment is deserving on a recent proposal to develop an aggregate energy elasticity for any entire system constituting an attempt to model the demand for energy (see Energy Modeling Forum[40]). Thus, for example, the Mid-range Energy Forecasting System (MEFS) of the Energy Information Administration should be made to produce an aggregate elasticity that can be compared to, say, the aggregate elasticity derived from the Brookhaven Energy Systems Optimization Model (BESOM) of the Brookhaven National Laboratory. The basis of the demand structure in MEFS consists of the demand models discussed previously, while BESOM has an analogous demand structure. The questions previously raised concerning the demand structures are still valid when separate sectors are examined. The important issue from the aggregate perspective is whether, in light of our theoretical/measurement considerations, such an aggregate elasticity makes any sense and truly approximates the overall system response to changes in energy prices.

In computing aggregate elasticities for MEFS, for example, prices of the various types of energy sources are perturbed by 10 percent (other factors held constant) and the resultant impact on the quantity demanded noted. For 1985 (based on the *Annual Report to Congress—1979* results) one finds a value on the order of -0.45. The first problem is in interpreting exactly what this means. A series of demand relationships were used initially to relate the quantity of specific energy types demanded to prices, economic activity, etc. If one ignores for the moment the problems inherent in measuring these demand relationships and focuses just on the perturbation issue, is it proper to lend any credence to the resulting elasticity when the demand system was not estimated as a system (i.e., accepted econometric techniques for estimating systems of equations were not contemplated, must less tried)? One finds a mixture of short-term and long-term elasticities in the various models, which leads to a nebulous interpretation of the aggregate number.

Beyond this issue for a given modeling system (and all existing ones that are subject to the criticism), there is the problem of interpreting the elasticity coefficients across sytems. This problem rests on the fact that the weighting scheme adopted (across consuming sectors or energy sources based on price, quantities, population, or whatever) will influence the computed value. Even if the elasticities of two systems are computed relative to the same *numéraire* (e.g., the total quantity of energy consumed), the base values will undoubtedly be different. One is then confronted with trying to compare values that are different in computation. There is no resolution to this.

INTERFUEL SUBSTITUTION

In addition to the concern for energy demand estimation is the issue of substitution of one type of energy for another. Measurement problems analogous to those previously mentioned exist in this instance as well. There is no need to dwell on them at length since they should be self-evident at this juncture.

As previously discussed, the possibility of substituting one energy type for another exists. This contention is reinforced when the energy share expenditures across regions in the United States are examined (see Table I.1). Interregional energy share differences are attributable to a number of factors including relative price differentials, economic activity (per capita income) differences, and characteristics unique to the region such as climate, industrial product composition, and demographic factors. Price and economic activity differences are especially important in the current analysis. Disparities arising due to differentials in price attest to the possibility of interfuel substitution and, hence, conservation of specific types of energy. Expenditure share variations arising because of

Tabel I.1.   Energy Expenditures Shares, 1978

Region	Coal Total	Oil Total	Natural Gas Total	Electrical Energy Total
1. New England	0.02	0.65	0.08	0.25
2. Middle Atlantic	0.08	0.52	0.12	0.28
3. East North Central	0.11	0.46	0.16	0.27
4. West North Central	0.06	0.52	0.16	0.26
5. South Atlantic	0.09	0.55	0.08	0.28
6. East South Central	0.12	0.50	0.10	0.28
7. West South Central	0.02	0.50	0.22	0.26
8. Mountain	0.04	0.57	0.14	0.25
9. Pacific	0.05	0.55	0.14	0.26

Source: U.S. Department of Energy

differences in the levels of economic activity provide a good basis on which to forecast the evolution of a region's energy consumption mix from its overall development configuration. Because of their policy implications, the price and secondarily the economic active impacts on energy choices are focused upon. It should be realized, however, that these factors alone cannot be expected to completely explain the observed differences.

The general approach to modeling interfuel substitution is that suggested by Christensen et al.,[41] Hudson and Jorgenson,[42] and Jorgenson and Berndt.[43] The nature of this approach is highlighted here with the specifics relegated to the appropriate chapters since there are some sector specific variations. Energy, E, is viewed together with other factors of production, Σ, as inputs into the production process where output is denoted by Q. This leads to the production function (defined for any sector):

$$Q = \Omega(E, \Sigma, t), \qquad (1.4)$$

where t denotes technological change. For given factor prices and a prespecified level of output, energy demand can be coincidentally determined with the other factors (assuming, of course, cost-minimizing behavior).

With the determination of the aggregate demand for energy by a given sector accomplished, interfuel substitution responses can be determined. A homogeneous energy aggregate is hypothesized that is solely a function of the various energy inputs. Thus, for example, with three types of energy, T_i, the energy aggregate is written as

$$E = \Omega_E(T_1, T_2, T_3). \tag{1.5}$$

The energy-type-specific determination occurs at this point.

The separation of the aggregate energy demand from the energy source specific demand is, because of methodological and data limitations, typical. Unfortunately this procedure imposes strong theoretical aggregation conditions that are unlikely to be satisfied. Berndt and Christenson,[44] for example, have demonstrated that a sufficient aggregation condition requires the weak separability of the energy aggregate. In order for weak separability to hold, common elasticities of substitution must exist between each energy type and the other factors of production. There is little choice but to proceed with the weak separability assumption, while realizing that it may impart a bias in the resultant estimates.

With a precise delineation of the functional forms for relationships (1.4) and (1.5), requisite parameter estimates can be obtained. They (the estimates) will provide local approximations to historical technology and behavioral considerations. If, however, the specification is to serve as a useful forecasting device, then the model must be well behaved over the entire price range. Consequently, even though the precise specification purports to be only a local approximation, it must be treated as offering an approximation over the relevant range of relative price variations. Specifically, by Shephard's lemma, energy inputs are nonnegative. Consequently, energy cost shares are either positive or zero. This is referred to as monotonicity. A second set of conditions that must be satisfied is the concavity of the cost function in input prices. This requires that the Hessian matrix be negative semidefinite. In the analysis, these conditions must be scrutinized.

OUTLINE OF THE STUDY

As indicated in the foregoing discussion, the primary concerns of this volume are with the determinants of the demand for energy in general and the demand for specific energy types in particular. It is critical to isolate the effects of prices, economic activity, and other factors. The effect of price in particular is reflected in factor substitution (i.e., energy for non-energy inputs) and in interfuel substitution. The impact of economic activity on energy demand emanates from the composition of GNP.

The approach to developing an energy demand model for the United States is to examine four sectors—the residential sector (including the residential, commercial, mining, agricultural, and governmental sectors), the industrial sector, the transportation sector, and electric utilities. Chapters 2 through 5 look at the details of empirically estimating substitution responses and quantifying income and price elasticities by taking into account, to the extent possible, the methodological problems discussed. The intent of the exposition in these chapters is to make the elements of commonality between sectors as explicit as possible in an effort to give an appreciation of the symmetry of the approach used in the modeling process. In addition to the issue of the magnitude of the substitution response of various forms of energy to changes in relative prices is the question of whether this response has remained stable over the sample horizon. Consequently, this is statistically tested for.

Data limitations prohibit making the estimation precisely conformable. Regional data exist for the residential and electric utility sectors. Two-digit SIC (Standard Industrial Classification) data are used in estimating the demand for energy in the industrial sector, while only U.S. aggregate data are obtainable for the transportation sector.

In Chapter VI the energy demand model is brought together into an integrated whole. The penultimate chapter focuses on the policy implication of the model. There is a pressing need for the distillation of the character of future energy demand and an assessment of the sensitivity of energy demand to variations in key uncertain parameters and assumptions. The focus here is on the longer run, and so the adjustment process is relegated to the background. There are uncertainties. This, coupled with the process of adaptation in the energy system, implies that the next 20 years will be a period of changing energy demand. The hope is that the analysis of the structure of energy demand will provide an approximate outline of the route to be followed. The final chapter addresses this issue.

NOTES AND REFERENCES

1. A correlation of 0.76 between first difference series for GNP and aggregate energy demand is observed.
2. See, e.g., C.J. Hitch, *Modeling Energy-Economy Interactions.* Washington, D.C.: Resources for the Future, 1977.
3. B. Netschert et al., contains more on this in "Competition in Energy Markets," in *Economics of Energy,* L.F. Grayson, (ed.). Princeton, N.J.: The Darwin Press, 1975.
4. U.S. Congress, *Power Plant Sitting and Environmental Protection.* Washington, D.C.: U.S. Government Printing Office, 1971.
5. S.D. Freeman, *Energy.* Chicago: Rand McNally and Company, 1975.
6. H.S. Houthakker, "Will There be an Energy Crisis," paper presented to the American Mining Conference, Pittsburgh, 1971.
7. W. Hogan, "Dimension of Energy Demand," in *Selected Studies in Energy,* H. Landsberg, (ed.). Cambridge, Mass.: Ballinger Publishing Company, 1980.
8. U.S. Department of Energy, *Demonstrated Reserve Base of Coal in the United States.* Washington, D.C.: U.S. Govrnment Printing Office, 1981.
9. National Petroleum Council, *Guide to National Petroleum Council Report on U.S. Energy Outlook.* Washington, D.C.: National Petroleum Council, 1973.
10. See A. Deaton and J. Muellbauer, *Economics and Consumer Behavior.* Cambridge, Cambridge University Press, 1980.
11. A. Marshall, *Principles of Economics.* 9th (variorum) ed. London, The Macmillan Company, 1920.
12. J.N. Keynes, *The Scope and Method of Political Economy.* New York: The Macmillan Company, 1891.
13. See J.A. Schumpeter, *History of Economic Analysis.* New York: Oxford University Press, 1954.
14. P.A. Samuelson, *Foundations of Economic Analysis.* Cambridge, Mass.: Harvard University Press, 1947.
15. Samuelson goes on to criticize elasticity expressions as being an actual nuisance in more complicated systems by converting symmetrical expressions into asymmetrical ones and hiding the definiteness of quadratic forms.
16. W.D. Nordhaus, *The Efficient Use of Energy Resources.* New Haven, Conn.: Yale University Press, 1979.
17. K.J. Arrow, *Essays in the Theory of Risk Bearing.* Chicago: Markham Publishing Company, 1971.
18. Throughout the discussion, data related issues are suppressed.
19. These issues are more comprehensively covered in applied treatises such as J.S. Cramer, *Empirical Econometrics.* Amsterdam: North-Holland

Publishing Company, 1971; M.D. Intrilligator, *Econometric Models, Techniques, and Applications.* Englewood Cliffs, N.J.: Prentice-Hall, Inc., 1978; and L. Phlips, *Applied Consumption Analysis.* Amsterdam: North-Holland Publishing Company, 1974.

20. H. Wold and L. Jureen, *Demand Analysis.* New York: John Wiley and Sons, Inc., 1953.

21. R. Stone, "Linear Expenditure System and Demand Analysis: An Application to the Pattern of British Demand." *Economic Journal 64:*511–527, 1954.

22. J.L. Bridge, *Applied Econometrics.* Amsterdam: North-Holland Publishing Company, 1971.

23. A. Zellner, "Statistical Analysis of Econometric Models." *Journal of the American Statistical Association* 74(367):628–643, 1979.

24. J.B. Ramsey, "Classical Model Selection Through Specification Error Tests," in *Frontiers in Econometrics* (P. Zerembka, ed.). New York: Academic Press, 1974.

25. L.D. Taylor, *The Demand for Energy: A Survey of Price and Income Elasticities.* University of Arizona, Processed, April 1976.

26. H.S. Houthakker, "New Evidence on Demand Elasticities." *Econometrica 33:*277–288, 1965.

27. R. Stone, "Linear Expenditure System and Demand Analysis: An Application to the Pattern of British Demand." *Economic Journal 64:*511–527, 1954.

28. F.M. Fisher, *The Identification Problem in Econometrics.* New York: McGraw-Hill Book Company, 1966.

29. N.D. Uri, "Price Expectations and the Demand for Electrical Energy." *Energy Systems and Policy 3:*73–83, 1979.

30. H.S. Houthakker and L.D. Taylor, *Consumer Demand in the United States.* Cambridge, Mass.: Harvard University Press, 1970.

31. Energy Information Administration, *Annual Report to Congress—1979.* Washington, D.C.: U.S. Government Printing Office, 1980.

32. Federal Energy Administration, *National Petroleum Product Supply and Demand 1975.* Washington, D.C.: U.S. Government Printing Office, 1975.

33. Short-Term Analysis Division, *Short-Term Energy Outlook, February 1980,* Energy Information Administration, Washington, February 1980.

34. A complete discussion is contained in E. Hirst and J. Carney, *The ORNL Engineering-Economic Model of Residential Energy Use,* ORNL/CON-24, Oak Ridge National Laboratory, Oak Ridge, Tenn.: 1976.

35. A development of the methodology is in J.R. Jackson, S. Cohn, J. Cope, and W.S. Johnson, *The Commercial Demand for Energy: A Disaggregated Approach,* Oak Ridge National Laboratory, Oak Ridge, Tenn.: April 1970.

36. M.L. Baughman and P.L. Joskow, "Energy Consumption and Fuel Choice by Residential and Commercial Consumers in the United States." *Energy Systems and Policy 1*(4):276–291, 1976.

37. A detail of the methodological and empirical development is given by

Synergy, Inc., *Demand Analysis System*. Washington, D.C.: Synergy, Inc., December 1979.

38. H.S. Houthakker and L.D. Taylor, *Consumer Demand in the United States.* Cambridge, Mass.: Harvard University Press, 1970.

39. The specifics are presented in D. Gantzer, *Mid-Range Energy Demand Forecasting in the Transportation Sector,* Office of Energy Use Analysis, Processed, August 1979.

40. Energy Modeling Forum, *Aggregate Elasticity of Energy Demand,* Energy Modeling Forum, Stanford University, January 1980.

41. L.R. Christensen, D.W. Jorgenson and L.J. Lau, "Transcendental Logarithmic Production Frontiers." *The Review of Economics and Statistics 55*(August):259–268, 1975.

42. E.A. Hudson and D. Jorgenson "U.S. Energy Policy and Economic Growth." *The Bell Journal of Economics and Management Science 5*(Autumn):461–514, 1974.

43. D.W. Jorgenson and E.R. Berndt, "Production Structure," in *Energy Resources and Economic Growth* by D.W. Jorgenson and H.S. Houthakker (ed.). Lexington, Mass.: Data Resources Inc., 1973.

44. E. Berndt and L. Christenson, "The Internal Structure of Functional Relationship." *The Review of Economic Studies 62*(July):403–410, 1963.

Chapter II

The Residential Demand for Energy

INTRODUCTION

The largest component of total energy consumption in 1978 was attributable to the residential sector. (Note that here the residential sector is a rather amorphous group including government, agriculture, mining, construction, and commercial users in addition to residential customers.) The relative roles of residential, commercial, agricultural, mining, construction, and governmental users vary greatly among regions in the United States. Hoch, for example, finds that for nine regions, residential use accounts for between 15 and 43 percent of the total energy consuhption for the sector. Commercial uses vary between 23 and 40 percent of the total and government accounts only for between 2 and 6 percent of the total.[1]

The residential sector has been the target of energy conservation measures in the United States. Conservation policies, however, are often designed in the absence of any reliable estimates of their likely long-run impact on use. In modeling this sector, the investigator is at a disadvantage in that the available data do not refer to a well-defined activity. The efficacy of conventional microeconomic theory is dampened as the theory of the consumer is not applicable to commercial, governmental, construction, mining, and agricultural users, nor is the notion of a firm's production function applicable to the residential component of consumption. As a consequence,

29

the model developed has its focus on deriving empirical relationships with consistent prior properties and reasonable explanatory powers while relegating the theoretical niceties to the hinterland.

This limitation in no way mitigates the importance of the residential sector as a significant part of total final energy consumption. As indicated in Table II.1, the residential sector accounts for at least 30 percent of final energy consumption in the various regions in the United States.

In identifying the determinants of aggregate energy consumption in the residential sector, one must consider income and price as well as the factors giving rise to interregional heterogeneity. The increase in the level of economic activity on a per capita basis is typically considered to be the most significant factor affecting higher per capita residential energy consumption.[2] An increasing level of economic activity lends to improved space conditioning (more and better heated and cooled homes), a larger assortment of energy-using appliances and equipment, etc. Variations in energy use across regions is likewise visible. Weather is the major factor affecting space conditioning requirements, which gives rise to a significant degree of interregional heterogeneity. The number of heating degree days[3] in the West South Central region is less than twice the number in the New England region. Consequently, the high proportion of residential energy consumption to total energy consumption in New England is due in part to climatic conditions. Thermal characteristics of houses in various regions also show a large degree of variability. As a result, even if energy prices were uniform across regions, there would still be regional variations in the use of energy.

The effect of energy prices on consumption is more difficult to describe. The substitution of energy for other goods and services is possible. Energy for space heating and cooling, for example, is substitutable for house size, insulation, and various other conservation initiatives. Thus, one finds houses in the northern regions of the United States on average better insulated than in the southern regions.[4]

There is also considerable variability in the fuel mix among regions. This is illustrated in Table II.1. The reasons for this lie in resource availability, relative prices, and interregional

Table II.1   Residential Energy Use, 1978

Region	Residential Energy Consumption / Total Final Energy Consumption	Residential Energy Expenditures / Total Energy Expenditures	Fuel Mix Expenditures			
			Coal / Total Energy	Natural Gas / Total Energy	Oil / Total Energy	Electrical Energy / Total Energy
1. New England	0.5098	0.6377	0.0003	0.2183	0.0683	0.7131
2. Middle Atlantic	0.4345	0.6094	0.0013	0.1367	0.0857	0.7763
3. East North Central	0.3845	0.5807	0.0018	0.0770	0.1426	0.7786
4. West North Central	0.3898	0.5882	0.0007	0.0512	0.1192	0.8289
5. South Atlantic	0.3549	0.5759	0.0006	0.0377	0.0484	0.9133
6. East South Central	0.3005	0.5431	0.0012	0.0319	0.0710	0.8959
7. West South	0.3764	0.5091	0.0001	0.0209	0.0867	0.8923
8. Mountain	0.3166	0.5314	0.0013	0.0293	0.0842	0.8852
9. Pacific	0.3790	0.5671	0.0003	0.0245	0.0967	0.8785

Source: Bureau of Mines, Department of Energy

heterogeneity (e.g., climatic differences) as well as the level of economic activity. This last consideration is especially relevant in that the environmental qualities of fuels (i.e., clean burning versus dirty fuels) become desirable and accessible coincident with the rising standard of living. As an example, electrical energy and gas are clean fuels requiring little maintenance by the consumer. Coal, on the other hand, is an extremely dirty fuel requiring manual loading into the furnace and ash removal. The substitution of other fuels for coal as per capita incomes have risen is dramatically illustrated by the drop in the coal expenditure share from more than 50 percent during the early decades of the twentieth century to less than 0.2 percent for the aggregate United States in 1978.

Interregional heterogeneity likewise is an important ingredient in the choice of fuels. Fuel mix varies depending on the relative importance of the various components of the residential sector. The type of energy required varies with each component. Thus, for example, in the agricultural sector oil (distillate fuel oil) is required for the operation of farm machinery. Regions such as the East North Central and West North Central, which are relatively more agrarian, would be expected to have a higher relative expenditure on oil.

Given these reflections, the objective here is to investigate the demand for energy in this amorphous residential sector. This investigation is a three-step process. First, the aggregate demand for energy is determined. Subsequently, the factors giving rise to variations in the mix of fuels are studied. Attention will focus on the elasticity of substitution between the various types of energy. Finally, the stability of the observed relationships is tested for and the appropriate policy implications drawn.

A MODEL OF AGGREGATE ENERGY DEMAND

The methodology adopted to model aggregate energy consumption is the traditional formulation based on price and economic activity variable.[5] The appropriateness of these factors is embedded in economic theory. Alternative approaches might be considered. For example, an indirect translog utility function decomposing total consumption expenditures into six categories (apparel, durable goods, food, transportation and communication, energy, and other) along the lines of Pindyck is possible.[6] These approaches were foregone. The principal reason is that due to the heterogeneous composition of the sector the functional form is not stable across regions while the more straightforward model designed to reflect interregional differences is stable (in the statistical sense). Moreover, data requirements in such an approach would be greatly multiplied, including time series information on the prices and expenditures on nonenergy commodities (e.g., apparel).

The focus of the investigation is on long-run relationships. (Note that because of this no short-run adjustment parameter is introduced.) As a result, the methodology used in the current analysis is the Houthakker–Taylor approach which suggests aggregate energy consumption per capita, E, is a linear-in-logarithms function of the level of economic well-being (measured as real per capita income), Y, and the price of energy relative to the price of all goods and services, P_e. Further, in the absence of adequate capital stock data, responses to energy price changes will be spread out over several years. Consequently, a distributed lag process is introduced in the case of the price of energy. To reflect interregional differences, a series of regional dummy variables is included defined along the lines suggested by Suits.[7] Finally, given the extreme importance of weather in influencing the consumption of energy,[8] both heating degree days [HDD] and cooling degree days [CDD] are used. The exact specification is thus:

$$E_t = \sum_{i=1}^{9} \alpha_i + \beta_1 Y_t + \beta_2[\text{HDD}] + \beta_3[\text{CDD}] + \sum_{j=1} \theta_j P_e(t-j), \quad (2.1)$$

where α_is, β_is, and θ_js are parameters to be estimated and the subscript t denotes the current period.

A priori one would expect the coefficient on economic well-being and the two weather variables to be positive. Thus, as the winter weather becomes more severe, the demand for space heating services and hence for energy increases. In fact, Darmstadter and colleagues note that space conditioning accounts for some 70–80 percent of household energy use.[9] The inclusion of temperature will serve to reflect interregional climatic effects. In the case of energy prices, it is well understood that changes in the price of energy will alter the utilization of the appliance stock in the current period. Additionally, as the price of energy increases relative to the price of capital (i.e., energy-using appliances and equipment) there will be a replacement of the existing (and hence implicitly less energy-efficient) appliances by relatively more energy-efficient appliances. Since the replacement process is spread out over several years, price changes in the current period would be expected to influence energy consumption several years hence.[10]

The data needed to estimate relationship (1.1) are available, although some manipulation is required. Data on natural gas price and the quantity consumed are available from the American Gas Association.[11] Analogous data for electrical energy price and quantity consumed come from the Edison Electric Institute.[12] The Bureau of Mines of the U.S. Department of Energy is the source of the data on oil price and consumption as well as on coal price and consumption.[13] The population data (to enable the computation of per capita energy consumption) and the regional personal income data together with the implicit price deflator were obtained from the Bureau of Economic Analysis, U.S. Department of Commerce. The weather data (population weighted by state) were provided by the National Oceanic and Atmospheric Administration. The time period is 1947 through 1978.

Per capita energy consumption was computed by adding all of the energy inputs, measured in British thermal units and applying the following thermal adjustment factors: coal, 0.20; natural gas, 0.70; oil, 0.60; electrical energy, 1.0.[14] The sum of the thermally adjusted regional energy consumption is then divided by population. The price of energy relative to other goods is computed by calculating a quantity weighted average energy price and dividing by the implicit price deflator.

The results of the estimation are given in Table II.2. Various lengths of the price lag were tried using the polynominal distributed lag technique of Almon.[15] A second-order lag using a cubic polynomial provided the best (in the statistical sense) fit. This is not meant to imply unequivocally that the effects of a price change are exhausted after two years—only that the identifiable, measurable effect dissipates after that period. The data were pooled across regions, and the estimates corrected for serial correlation.

Table II.2 Aggregate Energy Consumption for the Residential Sector

Parameter[1]	Estimate[2]
α_1	3.8152
	(1.4260)
α_2	3.9465
	(1.3977)
α_3	3.9781
	(1.5025)
α_4	3.9290
	(1.5911)
α_5	3.9654
	(1.4604)
α_6	3.8350
	(1.3698)
α_7	3.9624
	(1.5241)
α_8	3.8114
	(1.7462)
α_9	3.8756
	(1.2119)
β_1	−0.1453
	(0.0250)
β_2	−0.1558
	(0.0413)
β_3	−0.0488
	(0.0093)
θ_1	1.1714
	(0.0247)
θ_2	0.1471
	(0.0704)
θ_3	0.1320
	(0.0612)
[3]	0.2631
	(0.1124)
$\bar{R}^2$	0.9942
D.W. Statistic[4]	1.96

Notes:

[1] α_1 - New England region, α_2 - Middle Atlantic region
α_3 - East North Central region, α_4 - West North Central region
α_5 - South Atlantic region, α_6 - East South Central region
α_7 - West South Central region, α_8 - Mountain region, α_9 - Pacific region
[2] Standard errors of estimates in parentheses
[3] Serial correlation coefficient
[4] Durbin Watson Statistic

The importance of economic well-being in explaining per capita energy consumption is quite transparent. Energy is a normal good and increased consumption is closely linked to rising per capita income. The income elasticity is 1.17, suggesting that as per capita income doubles energy consumption slightly more than doubles. This is within the range typically obtained by other investigators (see Taylor's survey[16]). Using a variety of data sets and estimating techniques, researchers typically find the income elasticity ranging between 0.68 and 1.98.

The energy price profile is significant and quite interesting. The effect of price changes in the current period is to reduce (increase) energy consumption by −0.15 for each 1 percent increase (decrease). The impact of price reaches its peak in the subsequent period when for each 1 percent change in price in the current period the quantity consumed per capita falls by 0.16 percent. The overall effect of a change in price by 1 percent alters consumption in the opposite direction by 0.35 percent. (Observe that the lag structure results because the nature of the polynomial fit through the coefficients.) This long-run elasticity is generally consistent with the values obtained by others. For example, Baughman and Joskow[17] find a price elasticity of −0.50, Nelson[18] obtains an estimate of −0.28, and Jorgenson suggests that −0.40 is the appropriate value.[19]

Weather is quite significant in affecting the quantity of energy consumed. One finds that, for example, a 1 percent increase in summer weather severity (as indicated by a rise in cooling degree days) increases energy consumption by 0.13 percent. This result is in accord with the value obtained by Uri[20] and roughly consistent with the estimate of Taylor and associates.[21]

FUEL SHARE EXPENDITURE DETERMINATION

Background

One approach to an exploration of the possibilities for interfuel substitution in the residential sector is to consider the issue as one of minimizing the costs of satisfying a given level of aggregate energy demand subject, of course, to the institutional constraints. The economic agents included in this minimizing process are commercial consumers, residential consumers, agriculture consumers, and the government. One of the institutional considerations is the role coal currently plays in satisfying aggregate energy demand. As already noted, it accounts for less than 0.2 percent of regional energy expenditures. Moreover, given its undesirability, the expectations are that by the mid-1980s it will all but disappear as a fuel source in the residential sector.[22] Given this likelihood, an energy cost function is hypothesized that depends on just the prices of oil, natural gas, and electrical energy:

$$P_E = \Omega(P_O, P_G, P_{EE}), \qquad (2.2)$$

where P_O, P_G, and P_{EE} denote the prices of oil, natural gas, and electrical energy, respectively.

It is desirable to specify a general functional form which has a minimal number of a priori restrictions. The translog price possibility frontier allows a large degree of generality since it places no restrictions on the Allen partial elasticities of substitution and can be viewed as a second-order approximation to any arbitrary twice-differentiable price possibility frontier.[23]

The translog price possibility frontier for the energy price aggregate is expressed as follows:

$$\log P_E = \alpha_O + \sum_i \alpha_i \log P_i \\ + \tfrac{1}{2} \sum_i \sum_j \gamma_{ij} \log P_i \log P_j \qquad (j = G, O, EE), \qquad (2.3)$$

where the α's and γ's are unknown parameters and G, O, and EE refer to prices of the fuels. In order to correspond to a well-behaved cost function, a price possibility frontier must be homogeneous of degree 1 in prices; that is, for a fixed-level aggregate energy consumption, total energy expenditures must increase proportionately when all fuel prices increase proportionately. This implies the following relationships among the parameters:

$$\sum_i \alpha_i = 1 \qquad (2.4)$$

and

$$\sum_i \gamma_{ij} = 0 \qquad (i, j = G, O, EE). \qquad (2.5)$$

A convenient feature of the price possibility frontier approach is that the derived demand functions for the fuels can be easily computed by partially differentiating relationship (2.3) with respect to the fuel prices; that is,

$$\frac{\partial P_E}{\partial P_i} = X_i. \tag{2.6}$$

This result, known as Shephard's lemma,[24] is conveniently expressed in logarithmic form for the translog price possibility frontier as follows:

$$\frac{\partial \log P_E}{\partial \log P_i} = \frac{P_i X_i}{\Sigma_j P_j X_j} = S_i \qquad (i, j = G, O, EE), \tag{2.7}$$

where S_i indicates the cost share of the ith fuel. The translog price possibility frontier yields the cost share equations as follows:

$$S_G = \alpha_G + \gamma_{GG} \log P_G + \gamma_{GO} \log P_O + \gamma_{GEE} \log P_{EE}; \tag{2.8a}$$

$$S_O = \alpha_O + \gamma_{OG} \log P_G + \gamma_{OO} \log P_O + \gamma_{OEE} \log P_{EE}; \tag{2.8b}$$

$$S_{EE} = \alpha_{EE} + \gamma_{EEG} \log P_G + \gamma_{EEO} \log P_O + \gamma_{EEEE} \log P_{EE}. \tag{2.8c}$$

Note that the cost shares sum to unity.

The application of Shephard's lemma implies that fuel prices are exogenously determined for the residential sector. Given this, actual fuel prices can be used in the estimation process without introducing the concern over simultaneous equation bias. The markets for natural gas and oil are nationwide and worldwide. The market for electrical energy is regulated. Consequently, residential consumption in a specific region has little discernible impact on the delivered prices of the fuels.

Uzawa[25] has shown that Allen partial elasticities[26] of substitution between fuels are given by the formula

$$\alpha_{ij} = \frac{\Omega_E \cdot \Omega_E^{ij}}{\Omega_E^i \cdot \Omega_E^j}, \tag{2.9}$$

where the superscripts on Ω_E indicate the partial differentiation of the cost function (2.3) with respect to the fuel prices. For the translog price possibility factor, we have

$$\sigma_{ii} = \frac{\gamma_{ii} + S_i^2 - S_i}{S_i^2} \tag{2.10a}$$

and

$$\sigma_{ij} = \frac{\gamma_{ij} + S_iS_j}{S_iS_j} \quad (i \neq j) \quad \text{for} \quad i, j = G, O, EE. \quad (2.10b)$$

Further, Allen has shown (see note 26) that the elasticities of substitution are related to the price elasticities of demand for the fuels, η_{ij}, as

$$\eta_{ij} = S_j\sigma_{ij} \quad (2.11)$$

This formulation assumes that $\Sigma_j \, \eta_{ij} = 0$ because of linear homogeneity in fuel prices.

The partial elasticities of substitution are invariant with regard to the ordering of the fuel input factors. Therefore $\sigma_{ij} = \sigma_{ji}$ although, in general, $\eta_{ij} \neq \eta_{ji}$.

Before proceeding it is instructive to reflect upon just what it is that is the objective of the estimation. The purpose here is to derive estimates of long-run regional interfuel substitution possibilities and estimates of the price elasticities of demand. The translog formulation is a means to that end, not an end in itself.

Estimation Procedure

It is feasible to estimate the parameters of the price-possibility frontier using ordinary least squares analysis. This technique is certainly attractive from the point of view of simplicity. It neglects, however, the additional information contained in the share equations, which are also easily estimable. Furthermore, even for a modest number of factor prices, the translog price possibility frontier has a large number of regressors which do not vary greatly across regions. Hence multicollinearity may be a problem, resulting in imprecise parameter estimates.

An alternative estimation procedure—and the approach used here—is to jointly estimate the cost share equations as a multivariate regression system. This procedure is satisfactory since the cost share equations include all the parameters of the price-possibility frontier except the constant, and no information is lost by not including the price-possibility frontier in the estimation procedure.

Additive disturbances are specified for each of the share

equations. Since the cost share equations are derived by differentiation, they do not contain the disturbance term from the cost function. It is assumed that the disturbances have a joint normal distribution. Following Zellner,[27] nonzero correlations across regions are allowed but zero correlations across time are imposed. However, his proposed estimation procedure is not operational for our model. The estimated disturbance covariance matrix required to implement Zellner's procedure is singular because the disturbances on the share equations must sum to zero for each region. The Zellner procedure can be made operational by deleting one of the share equations from the system. However, the estimates so obtained will not be invariant to which equation is deleted.

Barten[28] has shown that maximum likelihood estimates of a system of share equations with one equation deleted are invariant no matter which equation is dropped. Kmenta and and Gilbert[29] have shown that iteration of the Zellner estimation procedure until convergence results in maximum likelihood estimates. Iterating the Zellner procedure is a computationally efficient method for obtaining maximum likelihood estimates, and this is the procedure employed here.

Data

The share equations are estimated with pooled annual data compiled by Census' region[30] for the period 1947 through 1978. The data were obtained from the sources previously enumerated for the aggregate demand model.

Note that regional coefficients were not included in the estimating equations because the estimation procedure captures interregional variation through the variance–covariance matrix.

Finally, natural gas curtailments became a significant consideration in 1973 with regard to aggregate energy consumption. They were not, however, significant for the residential sector.

Empirical Results

The maximum likelihood estimates are invariant no matter which equation is omitted. Consequently, Eqs. (2.8a) and (2.8c) were estimated and the coefficient estimates of (2.8b) derived from these. Linear homogeneity in fuel prices [i.e., constraints (2.4) and (2.5)] has been imposed. Additional regularity conditions which the price possibility frontier must satisfy in order to correspond to a well-behaved cost structure are montonicity and convexity in fuel prices. Sufficient conditions for these are positive fitted cost shares and negative definiteness of the bordered Hessian matrix of the price possibility frontier. These conditions are met at most observations for the model estimated, hence it is concluded that the estimated price possibility frontier represents a well-behaved cost structure.

Serial correlation, as with most time series models, proved to be a problem and hence had to be corrected for in each estimated share equation.

One additional issue presents itself: Are the parameters on the share equations symmetric? That is, does $\gamma_{ij} = \gamma_{ji}$? To test for symmetry, which implies that an increase in the price of fuel j will affect the expenditure share on fuel i to the same extent as a rise in the price of fuel i affects the expenditure on fuel j, a Quandt test is employed. The test consists of the following steps: Denote the determinants of the unrestricted and restricted estimates of the disturbance covariance matrix by $|\hat{\Sigma}_u|/|\hat{\Sigma}_r|$ when Eqs. (2.8a) and (2.8c) are estimated. The likelihood ratio becomes

$$\beta = \left(\frac{|\Sigma_u|}{|\Sigma_r|}\right)^{-T/2}, \tag{2.12}$$

where T is the number of observations. The hypothesis is tested using the fact that $-2 \log \beta$ has a chi-square distribution with degrees of freedom equal to the number of independent restrictions being imposed.[31] The test was performed with the null hypothesis being that symmetry holds. The determinant of the unconstrained covariance matrix was 167.283 while the determinant of the constrained covariance matrix was 167.190, indicating that the null hypothesis cannot be rejected at the 95 percent level.

Moreover, a preliminary examination of the results suggested that the serial correlation coefficient was equal across share equations. This constraint was imposed and the Quandt test employed. Assuming that symmetry is valid, the serial correlation constrained determinant was 167.086, suggesting that the effect of serial correlation is the same across share equations.

As a result of these two tests, the reported empirical estimates impose the symmetry constraint and equality of serial correlation constraint across share equations. The results are given in Table II.3. All of the estimates are significantly different than zero at the 95 percent level, leading to the conclusion that price elasticities and elasticities of substitution are not zero.

Table II.3 Parameter Estimates for
the Translog Fuel Expenditure
Shares Model

Parameter	Estimate[1]
α_G	0.1351 (0.0624)
α_O	0.0288 (0.0140)
α_{EE}	0.8361 (0.1708)
γ_{GG}	−0.0812 (0.0123)
γ_{OO}	0.0860 (0.0397)
γ_{EEEE}	−0.0364 (0.0171)
γ_{GO}	0.0654 (0.0247)
γ_{GEE}	0.0158 (0.0054)
γ_{OEE}	0.0206 (0.0104)
ρ^2	0.5965 (0.1077)

Notes:
[1] Standard errors of estimates in parentheses
[2] Serial correlation coefficient

Estimates of the average regional elasticities of substitution for the period 1947–1978 based upon cost shares are presented in Table II.4, and average regional price elasticities of demand over the period are presented in Table II.5. Own-price elasticities should be negative and cross-price elasticities should be positive. This is precisely the pattern that evolves. Note that the computed values are fairly representative of the last few years, given the relatively stable nature of the cost shares.

One observes a wide variation in regional price elasticities of demand in Table II.5. The differences are attributable to the fuel share composition within that region. Fox example, the New England region, with the highest cost share of natural gas in 1978 (22 percent), has the most inelastic demand for natural gas (-0.45), whereas the West South Central region, with a cost share of 2 percent, has a price elasticity of -1.90. The results follow from the properties of Eqs. (2.10a), (2.10b), and (2.11c), and the negative estimated coefficients for γ_{GG}, γ_{OO}, and γ_{EEEE}.

Residential energy consumers in the various regions are truly responding to price changes, though the response is not equal in both equations. This arises primarily because of the institutional constraints and technology involved in changing from one fuel to another. Take as an example the West South Central region, where it is much easier to shift from oil to natural

Table II.4 Regional Elasticities of Substitution for the Period 1947–1978

	Region	σ_{GG}	σ_{OO}	σ_{EEEE}	σ_{GO}	σ_{GEE}	σ_{OEE}
1.	New England	-1.17	-2.63	-0.43	1.94	0.76	0.99
2.	Middle Atlantic	-1.76	-2.49	-0.39	-1.72	-0.70	-0.77
3.	East North Central	-3.42	-1.04	-0.36	1.50	0.43	0.29
4.	West North Central	-3.77	-1.17	-0.29	1.47	0.49	0.36
5.	South Atlantic	-4.69	-4.31	-0.19	1.02	0.74	0.64
6.	East South Central	-4.75	-2.54	-0.24	0.90	0.61	0.37
7.	West South Central	-7.42	-2.42	-0.25	0.47	0.59	0.33
8.	Mountain	-6.91	-2.50	-0.37	0.56	0.62	0.59
9.	Pacific	-7.03	-3.01	-0.28	0.50	0.57	0.66
	Total United States	-1.85	-2.11	-0.35	1.02	0.62	0.54

Table II.5 Regional Price Elasticities of Demand for the Period 1957–1978

Region	η_{GG}	η_{OO}	η_{EEEE}	η_{GO}	η_{GEE}	η_{OOO}	η_{OEE}	η_{EEG}	η_{EEO}
1. New England	−0.45	−1.18	−0.92	0.63	0.21	0.54	0.57	0.29	0.68
2. Middle Atlantic	−0.54	−0.90	−0.74	0.59	0.34	0.52	0.64	0.40	0.67
3. East North Central	−0.67	−0.77	−0.73	0.72	0.19	0.68	0.51	0.22	0.49
4. West North Central	−0.78	−0.83	−0.68	0.50	0.12	0.31	0.47	0.19	0.59
5. South Atlantic	−0.84	−1.22	−0.53	0.96	0.67	0.87	0.79	0.49	0.64
6. East South Central	−0.85	−0.99	−0.50	0.72	0.61	0.74	0.21	0.54	0.30
7. West South Central	−1.90	−0.92	−0.57	0.58	0.37	0.27	0.61	0.48	0.47
8. Mountain	−1.41	−1.00	−0.68	0.23	0.33	0.17	0.39	0.34	0.42
9. Pacific	−1.23	−0.80	−0.65	0.39	0.45	0.42	0.74	0.38	0.61
Total United States	−1.01	−0.92	−0.71	0.64	0.41	0.55	0.63	0.46	0.59

gas (which accounted for 9 percent of fuel expenditures in 1978) as opposed to reversing the process by shifting from natural gas to oil because of the availability consideration. The cross-price elasticity in the former case is 0.58, as opposed to 0.27 in the latter case. In the East South Central region, on the other hand, the cross-price elasticities are of roughly equal size, with the shift between fuels being more clearly dictated by relative price changes than by the ease with which the change can be made.

What is the mechanism through which the observed interregional interfuel substitution occurs? First, the absolute decline in the consumption of a specific type of energy is accomplished by improving the thermal integrity of the existing stock of buildings and houses. Thus, by adding insulation, storm windows, storm doors, caulking, etc., one can save upwards of 30 percent on energy consumption.[32]

Increases in fuel prices relative to the price of energy-using appliances and equipment provide the incentive to replace the existing stock with appliances that are more energy efficient. Legislatively mandated appliance efficiency standards have provided the incentive to improve some appliance efficiencies by 20 percent.[33]

Finally, changing relative fuel prices alter the relative marginal costs of operating various appliances and equipment using different fuels and hence provide an incentive to switch to the lower-cost fuel by either retrofitting or replacing the existing stock of appliances. Moreover, new commercial and residential structures opt for the least cost fuel giving an appearance of overall fuel substitution in the form of relative expenditure shifts. Thus, for example, for the Pacific region in 1978, where natural gas was relatively less expensive than the other fuels, 57 percent of all the new home construction relied upon natural gas for space heating and cooking. On the other hand, in the New England region, where oil is most expensive, only 40 percent of new homes in 1978 were built to use oil for space heating. For the aggregate United States in 1978, 52 percent of new home construction used electrical energy for space conditioning and cooking, 37 percent utilized natural gas, and 11 percent used oil.[34]

The estimates in Table II.5 provide a basis for the calculation of average elasticities for all regions. Long-run own-price elasticities for the entire United States are -1.01, -0.92, and -0.71 for natural gas, oil, and electrical energy, respectively. These figures are comparable to price elasticity estimates found by Griffin[35] for 20 other countries; they are also fairly consistent with estimates found in other studies that use cross-section or pooled cross-section and times series data,[36] but they are somewhat larger than the estimates resulting from pure time series analysis.[37] If the results presented here are true, the policy significance is of great importance.

Time series analyses in particular have tended to find oil demand to be very inelastic. For example, Nissen and Knapp,[38] recently updated by the U.S. Department of Energy,[39] estimate the price elasticity of demand for energy for the combined residential sector as -0.27, -0.37, and -0.33 for natural gas, oil, and electrical energy, respectively. Comparison of the results derived here and those of the U.S. Department of Energy is particularly interesting since it tends to confirm the suspicion that the earlier pure time series approach captured only a portion of the long-run price response in situations involving long periods for appliance and equipment stock turnover.

As previously observed, a nice theoretical property of the translog formulation is that the sum of own- and cross-price elasticities among fuels is zero. It is instructive to consider the magnitude of the cross-price elasticities in order to determine the main channels of interfuel substitution. Table II.5 reports these elasticities. The effect of higher oil prices, say, will create an approximately equal stimulus to both electrical energy and natural gas consumption.

The aforementioned U.S. Department of Energy study of the residential sector provides a basis for comparison of cross-price elasticities as well. It finds the elasticity of demand for natural gas with respect to the price of oil to be 0.003 and the elasticity of demand for electrical energy with respect to the price of oil to be 0.05. The elasticity of the demand for oil with respect to the price of natural gas is 0.008. In all cases, the results obtained here indicate comparatively greater interfuel substitution effects.

TESTING FOR MODEL STABILITY

Major attention has focused on the demand for fuel inputs in the residential sector. Of major concern in the context of drawing meaningful inferences over the historical period as well as over any forecast horizon is whether the observed relationships (i.e., price elasticities) are stable. (Stability is defined in the statistical sense of the estimated coefficients of the explanatory variables remaining constant over time.) Policy inferences are made on the basis of past behavior. If the functional relationship has been subject to change, then necessarily the inferences will be, at least in part, unsatisfactory.

The purpose of this section is to examine the question of the existence of a stable demand for fuel inputs utilizing a statistical test developed by Brown and colleagues.[40] The approach is adopted in preference to others available (e.g., the Chow test[41]) because it does not require prior knowledge of the shifts, but rather tests for the presence of such occurrences over the sample period. To give an appreciation of this test, it will now be briefly discussed. A way of investigating the time variation of a regression coefficient is to fit the regression on a short segment of n successive observations and to move this segment along the series. A significance test for constancy based on this approach is derived from the results of regressions based on nonoverlapping time segments. The method relies on a test statistic which equals the difference between the sum of squared residuals of the entire sample less the cumulative sum of squared residuals of the nonoverlapping segments. The null hypothesis that the regression relationship is constant over time implies that the value of the test statistic is distributed as F. Specifically, consider the time segments for a moving regression of length $n - (1, n)$, $[(n + 1), (2n)]$, $\ldots, [(p - 1)n + 1, T]$, where p is the integral part of T/n and the variance ratio considered (i.e., the homogeneity statistic) is

$$\omega = \frac{T - kp}{kp - k} \frac{S(1, T) - \Delta}{\Delta}, \qquad (2.13)$$

where k is the number of regressors, $\Delta = \{S(1, n) + [S(n + 1), 2n] + \cdots + [(pn - n + 1), T]\}$, and $S(r, s)$ is the residual sum of squares from the regression calculated for observations t = r to s inclusive. This is equivalent to the usual "between groups over within groups" ratio of mean squares and under H_0 is distributed as $F(kp - k, T - kp)$.

Relying on the foregoing discussion, the objective is to explicitly test for the stability of the demand for fuel in the residential sector over the period 1947 through 1978. Dividing the data into 32 equal-length intervals (i.e., p = 32 and n = 9) allows for the computation of the test statistic for each of the share equations. What is done is equivalent to pooling across all nine regions for a given year and then examining the stability across years. As noted, one of the equations must be deleted, and as before the oil equation was selected.

The computed value of ω via Eq. (2.13), i.e., the test statistic for the two share equations, is given in Table II.6. The results are quite conclusive. Neither the equation for the demand for natural gas nor the equation for the demand for electrical energy by the residential sector is unstable for the period 1947 through 1978.

The implications of these results are clear and permit us to estimate the demand for energy by residential consumers. Events over the past three decades have left virtually unchanged the demand for natural gas and electrical energy (and implicitly the demand for oil). That is, for the factor inputs, the relative importance of the price of natural gas, the price of oil, and the price of electrical energy in influencing the share of total expenditures (and hence demand) has remained constant.

One must be careful, however, to avoid inferring that the relative quantities of natural gas, oil, and electrical energy demanded have remained unchanged. Our estimated results

Table II.6 Computed Value of the Stability Test Statistic ω

Share Equation	Computed Value of ω	Tabulated Critical Value[1]
1. Natural Gas	0.8645	1.32
2. Electrical Energy	1.0710	1.32

Note:
[1] That is, $F_{0.05}$ (124,160)

clearly show that the price of each fuel has influenced its expenditure share. Thus, an increase in the price of oil does indeed lead to an increase in the quantity of natural gas consumed. The magnitude of this response for each fuel in the aggregate remained unaltered over the sample period. Another way of expressing this is that the share elasticities for the fuels did not vary.

CONCLUSION

The residential sector as defined here is a substantial consumer of energy in the United States. The heterogeneous composition of the sector complicates modeling the demand for energy. After reflecting the particular nuances introduced by differing thermal characteristics of the various fuels, we find an income elasticity slightly in excess of 1 and a price elasticity of demand of approximately -0.35. The results are not inconsistent with other studies done for the United States.

A translog fuel share model yields some significant and interesting conclusions. Support is lent to the contention that consumers are responding to the relative changes in fuel prices by altering their energy consumption patterns.

Finally, the question of stability is addressed. The results are conclusive suggesting that the demand for natural gas, oil, and electrical energy have remained virtually constant over the past three decades.

NOTES AND REFERENCES

1. I. Hoch, *Energy Use in the United States by State and Region.* Washington, D.C.: Resources for the Future, 1978.
2. L.D. Taylor, "The Demand for Energy—A Survey of Price and Income Elasticities," in *International Studies in the Demand for Energy*, W. Nordhaus (ed.). Amsterdam: North-Holland Publishing Company, 1978.
3. A degree day is a unit measuring the extent to which the outdoor mean (average of maximum and minimum) daily dry-bulb temperature falls below or above a base of 65°F.
4. U.S. Department of Commerce, *Characteristics of Housing: 1979.* Washington, D.C.: U.S. Government Printing Office, 1979.
5. H.S. Houthakker and L.D. Taylor, *Consumer Demand in the United States.* Cambridge, Mass.: Harvard University Press, 1970.
6. R.S. Pindyck, "International Comparison of the Residential Demand for Energy." *European Economic Review 13:*123–140, 1980.

7. D.B. Suits, "Use of Dummy Variables in Regression Equations." *The Journal of the American Statistical Association 52:*548–551, 1957.

8. N.D. Uri, "Quantifying the Regional Impact of Weather Variations." *The Review of Regional Studies 7:*87–96, 1977.

9. J. Darmstadter, J. Dunkerley and J. Alterman, *How Industrial Societies Use Energy.* Baltimore, Md.: Johns Hopkins University Press, 1977.

10. E. Hirst and J. Carney, *The ORNL Engineering-Economic Model of Residential Energy Use.* Oak Ridge, Tenn.: Oak Ridge National Laboratory, 1975.

11. American Gas Association, *Gas Facts.* Washington, D.C.: American Gas Association, annual.

12. Edison Electric Institute, *Statistical Yearbook.* New York: Edison Electric Institute, annual.

13. Bureau of Mines, *Mineral Industries Yearbook.* Washington, D.C.: U.S. Government Printing Office, annual.

14. W.D. Nordhaus, "The Demand for Energy: An International Perspective." W.D. Nordhaus, (ed.), *The Demand for Energy: An International Perspective.* Amsterdam: North-Holland Publishing Company, 1978.

15. S. Almon, "The Distributed Lag Between Capital Appropriation and Expenditures." *Econometrica 33:*178–196, 1965.

16. L.D. Taylor, "The Demand for Energy: A Survey of Price and Income Elasticities," *The Demand for Energy: An International Perspective,* W. Nordhaus (ed.). Amsterdam: North-Holland Publishing Co., 1978.

17. M. Baughman and P. Joskow, "Interfuel Substitution in the Consumption of Energy in the United States," MIT Energy Laboratory Working Paper, 1974.

18. J.P. Nelson, "The Demand for Space Heating." *The Review of Economics and Statistics 57:*123–136, 1975.

19. D.W. Jorgenson, "Consumer Demand for Energy," in *The Demand for Energy: An International Comparison,* W. Nordhaus (ed.). Amsterdam: North-Holland Publishing Company, 1978.

20. N.D. Uri, "Quantifying the Regional Impact of Weather Variations." *The Review of Regional Studies 7:*87–96, 1977.

21. L.D. Taylor, P. Verlager, and G. Blattenberger, *The Residential Demand for Energy.* Palo Alto, Calif.: The Electric Power Research Institute, 1978.

22. Department of Energy, *Annual Report to Congress,* Volume 3. Washington, D.C.: U.S. Government Printing Office, 1980.

23. L.R. Christensen, D.W. Jorgenson and L.J. Lau, "Transcendental Logarithmic Production Frontiers." *The Review of Economics and Statistics 55*(February):28–45, 1973.

24. R.W. Shephard, *Cost and Production Functions.* Princeton, N.J.: Princeton University Press, 1963.

25. H. Uzawa, "Production Function with Constant Elasticities of Substitution." *The Review of Economics and Statistics 44*(October):291–299, 1962.

26. R.G.D. Allen, *Mathematical Analysis for Economists*. London: Macmillan and Company, 1938.

27. A. Zellner, "An Efficient Method of Estimating Seemingly Unrelated Regression and Tests for Aggregation Bias." *Journal of the American Statistical Association 57*(June):348–368, 1962.

28. A.P. Barten, "Maximum Likelihood Estimation of a Complete System of Demand Equations." *European Economic Review 1*(Fall):7–73, 1969.

29. J. Kmenta and R.F. Gilbert, "Small Sample Properties of Alternative Estimators of Seemingly Unrelated Regressions." *Journal of the American Statistical Association 63*(December):1180–1200, 1968.

30. The regional classification is as follows: (1) New England (Maine, New Hampshire, Vermont, Massachusetts, Rhode Island, Connecticut); (2) Middle Atlantic (New York, New Jersey, Pennsylvania); (3) East North Central (Ohio, Indiana, Illinois, Michigan, Wisconsin); (4) West North Central (Minnesota, Iowa, Missouri, North Dakota, South Dakota, Nebraska, Kansas); (5) South Atlantic (Delaware, Maryland and the District of Columbia, Virginia, West Virginia, North Carolina, Georgia, Florida); (6) East South Central (Arkansas, Louisiana, Oklahoma, Texas); (8) Mountain (Montana, Idaho, Wyoming, Colorado, New Mexico, Arizona, Utah, Nevada); and (9) Pacific (Washington, Oregon, California).

31. S. Goldfeld and R.E. Quandt, *Nonlinear Methods in Econometrics*. Amsterdam: North-Holland Publishing Company, 1972.

32. U.S. Department of Energy, *Solar Energy Objectives*. Washington, D.C.: U.S. Government Printing Office, 1980.

33. Office of Conservation and Solar Energy, *Strategy Papers*. Washington, D.C.: U.S. Government Printing Office, 1980.

34. U.S. Department of Commerce, *Characteristics of Housing*. Washington, D.C.: U.S. Government Printing Office, 1978.

35. J.M. Griffin, *Energy Conservation in the OECD: 1980 to 2000*. Cambridge, Mass.: Ballinger Publishing Company, 1979.

36. See, for example, R. Halvorsen, "Residential Demand for Energy." *Review of Economics and Statistics 57*:221–231, 1975; W.S. Chern, *Energy Demand and Interfuel Substitution in the Combined Residential and Commercial Sector*. Oak Ridge, Tenn.: Oak Ridge National Laboratory, 1976; W. Liu, E. Hirst, S. Cohn, *Fuel Choices in the Household Sector*. Oak Ridge, Tenn.: Oak Ridge National Laboratory, 1976; L.D. Taylor, G.P. Verlager, G. Blattenberger, *The Residential Demand for Energy*. Palo Alto, Calif.: Electric Power Research Institute, 1978.

37. For example, E.R. Berndt and G.C. Watkins, "A Residential and Commercial Energy Demand Model." *Canadian Journal of Economics 15*:21–40, 1978.

38. D. Nissen and D. Knapp, "A Regional Model of Interfuel Substitution," in *Energy: Mathematics and Models*, F. Roberts, (ed.). Philadelphia: SIAM, Inc. 1976.

39. U.S. Department of Energy, *Annual Report to Congress*, Volume 3. Washington, D.C.: U.S. Government Printing Office, 1980, pp. 332–333.

40. R.L. Brown, J. Durbin and J.M. Evans, "Techniques for Testing the Constancy of Regression Relationships Over Time." *Journal of the Royal Statistical Society 37:*149–163, 1975.
41. G. Chow, "Tests of Equality Between Two Sets of Coefficients in Two Linear Regressions." *Econometrica 28*(July):591–605, 1960.

Chapter III

The Industrial Demand
for Energy

INTRODUCTION

Measuring the demand for energy and the extent of interfuel substitution in the industrial sector is a challenging proposition. Given the relative importance of this sector to overall energy consumption (it accounted for 17 percent of total consumption in 1978), the degree to which fuels can be substituted in the production process is an essential ingredient in price-induced conservation. Moreover, there is the question of whether just various forms of energy are substitutable or whether in a larger context energy is substitutable for other factors of production.[1] The implication of this is significant. If energy and capital are substitutes, then any of the myriad of policies that foster accelerated replacement investment (e.g., accelerated depreciation, increased investment tax credits) will serve to reduce gross energy consumption. Alternatively, if energy and labor are substitutes, then increases in wages due, for example, to increased unionization and the attendant upward wage pressure will lead to expanded energy consumption.

In addition to the issue of factor substitutability, interfuel substitution possibilities among coal, natural gas, oil (distillate fuel oil and residual fuel oil), and electrical energy raise a set of related questions: Do variations in relative fuel prices account for some of the observed differences in fuel mixes across industries? Or are the observed differences solely the result of technological constraints?

53

The relative importance of industrial energy consumption at the two-digit SIC (Standard Industrial Classification) to aggregate U.S. energy consumption in 1978 is given in Table III.1. There is considerable variation. In part the differences reflect the technological differences between industries. For example, in the primary metals industries (SIC 33) and the stone, clay, and glass products industries (SIC 32) there is considerably larger consumption of energy as a boiler fuel needed in the manufacturing process than in other processes. Moreover, the size of output (measured as the value of goods produced) gives rise to some of the observed variation. Thus, for example, output of the lumber and wood products industries (SIC 24) was slightly more than twice that of the furniture and fixtures industries (SIC 25).

Not only are the interindustry effects reflected here but also intraindustry differences are quite important.[2] To some extent, the high proportion of industrial energy consumption is due to the presence of energy-intensive four-digit industries within the two-digit classification. Thus, for example, the primary metals industries are energy intensive (where energy intensity is measured by total energy consumption divided by value added) due to the energy intensity of SIC 3312 (blast furnaces and steel mills), whereas the stone, clay, and glass products industries reflect the high-energy intensity of SIC 3259 (structural clay products). Both inter- and intraindustry differences persist over time. Nevertheless, to the degree that the price of energy relative to the price of other factors of production affects energy consumption, the increasing relative price of energy will change future energy consumption patterns. Consequently, the technological effects must be differentiated from the price effects. In the following section, this issue of energy substitution between factors of production is critically examined. Using the conclusions from this, a model is formulated and estimated to forecast aggregate industrial energy consumption.

There is a wide spectrum of variation in fuel mixes between industries as demonstrated for 1978 in Table III.1. The expenditure on coal, for example, ranges from 3 percent in SIC 33 (petroleum and coal products) to 34 percent in SIC 26

Table III.1. Energy Consumption in the Industrial Sector, 1978

Industry	2-digit SIC Energy Consumption / Total U.S. Energy Consumption	Fuel Mix Expenditures in the Industrial Sector			
		Coal Total	Natural Gas Total	Oil Total	Electrical Energy Total
1. Food and Kindred Products (SIC 20)	0.0126	0.16	0.22	0.16	0.46
2. Tobacco Products (SIC 21)	0.0003	0.27	0.07	0.13	0.53
3. Textile Mill Products (SIC 22)	0.0044	0.18	0.07	0.14	0.61
4. Apparel, Other Textile Products (SIC 23)	0.0008	0.10	0.07	0.16	0.67
5. Lumber and Wood Products (SIC 24)	0.0033	0.07	0.08	0.33	0.52
6. Furniture and Fixtures (SIC 25)	0.0006	0.18	0.10	0.08	0.64
7. Paper and Allied Products (SIC 26)	0.0174	0.34	0.15	0.19	0.32
8. Printing and Publishing (SIC 27)	0.0011	0.03	0.11	0.08	0.78
9. Chemicals and Allied Products (SIC 28)	0.0405	0.20	0.18	0.07	0.55
10. Petroleum and Coal Products (SIC 29)	0.0173	0.03	0.02	0.62	0.33
11. Rubber, Misc. Plastics Products (SIC 30)	0.0032	0.18	0.07	0.13	0.62
12. Leather, Leather Products (SIC 31)	0.0003	0.19	0.08	0.17	0.56
13. Stone, Clay, Glass Products (SIC 32)	0.0164	0.22	0.37	0.12	0.29
14. Primary Metals Industries (SIC 33)	0.0319	0.12	0.12	0.22	0.54
15. Fabricated Metal Products (SIC 34)	0.0051	0.06	0.22	0.15	0.57
16. Machinery, Except Electrical (SIC 35)	0.0044	0.12	0.14	0.13	0.61
17. Electric, Electronic Equipment (SIC 36)	0.0031	0.11	0.14	0.09	0.66
18. Transportation Equipment (SIC 37)	0.0051	0.14	0.11	0.10	0.65
19. Instruments, Related Products (SIC 38)	0.0010	0.19	0.11	0.15	0.55
20. Miscellaneous Mfg. Industries (SIC 39)	0.0006	0.09	0.12	0.19	0.60

Source: Annual Survey of Manufacturers

(paper and allied products). Intraindustry differences in the four-digit SIC output mix explains most of this observation.

Industries that require a relatively clean fuel (e.g., food and kindred products and stone, clay, and glass) rely more heavily on natural gas and electrical energy. Electrical energy is desirable, further, because of its high thermal efficiency.

In the aggregate, considerable variation across two-digit SIC industries is evinced. As a result, a translog fuel-share model is used to try to capture the quantitative magnitude of interfuel substitution.

FACTOR SUBSTITUTABILITY

Introductory Comments

Recent years have seen a renewed interest in the study of factor substitutability and complementarity in the production process. Myriad inputs typically enter a firm's production process. Since a firm tends to choose that bundle of inputs that minimizes the total cost of producing a given level of output, the derived demand for inputs depends on the level of output, the substitution possibilities among inputs allowed by the existing technology, and the relative price of the inputs.

One important impetus for looking more intensively at factor substitutability and complementarity has been their potentially profound impact on the production process and the attendant implications for employment.[3] To the extent that energy has no substitutes then a reduction in its availability will result in inflation and a significant reduction in the level of employment. In this regard the impact of the Arab oil embargo on the U.S. economy in the 1974–1975 period is still not well understood because the relationship between factor inputs in the production process are not well understood. A large number of studies exist purporting to measure the degree of factor substitutability and complementarity using time series data, cross-section data, and pooled data. Berndt and Wood[4] provide a nice summary of the findings, and the interested reader is referred to these articles. The most interesting result of these studies is the contradictory evidence regarding substitution possibilities in general and substitution possibilities between energy and capital in particular.

It has been suggested that the conflicting evidence might be explained in a number of ways, including differing data sets and approaches to measuring factor input quantities and prices, as well as varied treatment of excluded inputs and distinctions between short-term and long-term elasticities. One explanation that has not been offered is that the estimates are so imprecise that they are picking up spurious relationships. That is, while the estimates show a substitution relationship, for example, between energy and capital, de facto no relationship exists, i.e., capital is not substitutable for energy. The implication of this is simply that a Leontief-type fixed coefficient production function would be a more appropriate representation of reality. What this issue reduces to is whether there is directional causality between the quantity of one factor and the price of another. Before providing any empirical investigation of this matter, a concise exposition of the theoretical rationale for anticipating changing factor intensities in the production process and a general discussion of directional causality are provided.

Theoretical Foundations

Consider the following example. Assume that a cost-minimizing competitive firm is initially in equilibrium with output at some equilibrium level and that the firm possesses a positive, twice-differentiable, strictly concave production function with four inputs (capital, K; labor, L; energy, E; and materials, M). Next, assume that the price of one of the factor inputs changes relative to the others (e.g., the price of energy rises). The total effect of this on the demand for the other factors can be decomposed into two parts: First, there will be the gross substitution effect resulting in a reduction in use of the factor with the higher relative price and an increase in the use of the other factors. (Note that this will always be the case—less of the input whose price increased and more of the other inputs.[5]) Second, there will be an expansion effect, which is the difference between the total effect and the gross substitution effect, where the total effect of such a price change results when the output of the production function is held constant and all inputs adjust to their new cost-minimizing levels. The magnitude of the expansion effect is dependent, of course, upon the marginal products of the factors of production.[6] It is possible for the expansion effect to dominate the gross substitution effect, with the result that one actually observes an increase in the use of the factor having the initial price increase. That is, it is possible that factors of production are gross substitutes but net complements. Whether net substitutability or complementarity exists depends on whether the gross substitution effect or the expansion effect is dominant. This is an empirical issue.

What is of relevance now is the extent to which we can sort out these effects. Myriad techniques exist to allow for such a determination. In other words, a large number of specifications are available that permit the estimation of elasticities of substitution for the factors of production. These specifications necessarily presuppose that the assumptions concerning the nature of the production function are correct. It need not be the case, however, that the factors of production are substitutable in the fashion assumed because the technology involved in the production process is prohibitive. Consequently, before hypothesizing a specific form of the production function, it is necessary to investigate whether there is any empirical basis to the notion that a change in the price of one factor of production will lead to a change in the utilization of all of the factors. This investigation will be carried out in the context of testing for directional causality. Before proceeding with the test it is useful to define precisely the concept of directional causality.

A Test for Directional Causality

From a given sample, typically one can construct many different models of causal influence, all of which are consistent with a given pattern of covariances among the variables. However, if enough identifying restrictions are available, one can test a particular causal ordering as a set of overidentifying restrictions. Unfortunately, the conditions allowing such a test are seldom met in practice.

C.W.J. Granger[7] has given a definition of a testable kind of causal ordering based on the notion that absence of correlation between past values of one variable X and that part of another variable Y which cannot be predicted from Y. More precisely, the time series Y is said to "cause" X relative to the universe U (U is a vector time series including X and Y as components) if and only if predictions of X(t) based on U(s) for all s < t are better than predictions based on all components U(s) except Y(s) for all s < t. In giving content to Granger's definition, it is necessary to assume that all time series are stationary, that only linear predictors are used, and that expected squared forecast error is the criterion for predictive accuracy.

Consider the stationary pair of stochastic processes X and Y. If X and Y are jointly purely linearly indeterministic, then

$$X_t = \sum_{j=1}^{m} a_j X_{t-j} + \sum_{j=1}^{m} b_j Y_{t-j} + \varepsilon_t$$

and (3.1)

$$Y_t = \sum_{j=1}^{m} c_j X_{t-j} + \sum_{j=1}^{m} d_j Y_{t-j} + \zeta_t,$$

where ε and ζ are mutually uncorrelated white noise (i.e., serially uncorrelated) processes and a, b, c, and d all vanish for t < 0.

The expressions of X and Y are the moving average representations of vector process

$$\begin{bmatrix} X \\ Y \end{bmatrix}$$

and are unique up to multiplication by a unitary matrix.

A useful result following from this definition is that Y does not cause X in Granger's definition if and only if a or b can be chosen identically 0.[8] (Sims denotes this as Theorem 2.)

This result gives an intuitive appreciation of Granger causality. If causality is from X to Y only, then of the two orthogonal white noises which make up X and Y, one is X itself "whitened" and the other is the error in predicting Y from current and past X, whitened. (A whitened variable is one which has been passed through a linear filter to make it a white noise.)

Granger has shown that if there is an autoregressive representation defined by (3.1), then the absence of causality running from Y to X is equivalent to all of the b_j's being zero. That is, causality runs only from X to Y if past Y does not influence current X. From this point it is not hard to show that when X and Y have an autoregressive representation, Y can be expressed as a distributed lag function of current and past X with a residual which is not correlated with any values of X, past or future, if and only if Y does not cause X in Granger's sense.

A regression of Y on current and past X can always be computed. But only in the special case where causality runs from X to Y can it be expected that no future values of X would enter the regression if allowed. Hence, there exists a practical statistical test for unidirectional causality: Regress Y on past and future values of X, taking account by generalized least squares of prefiltering of the serial correlation. Then if causality runs from X to Y only, future values of X in the regression should have coefficients insignificantly different from zero as a whole.

It is instructive to reflect on precisely what is being done with this test. The definition of causality is based entirely on the predictability of some series, say X. If another series, Y, contains information in past terms that helps in the prediction of X and if this information is contained in no other series used in the prediction, then Y is said to cause X. The flow of time clearly plays a central role in these definitions. It also follows from the notion of causality that a purely deterministic series, that is, a series which can be predicted exactly from its past terms such as a nonstochastic series, cannot be said to have any causal influences other than its own past.

The definition of causality employed implies that Y is causing X provided that one or more of the coefficients on the Y term in the first portion of relationship (3.1) is not zero (i.e., at least one b_j is different from zero). Similarly, X is causing Y if some c_j is not zero. If both of these events occur, there is said to be a feedback relationship between X and Y. It is demonstrated by Granger that this definition is identical to that discussed here. Because of the complexity of the proof, that demonstration is not reproduced. Additionally, the presumption that instantaneous causality is absent is also made.[9]

Finally, the consideration should be made as to whether the bivariate model underlying the analysis would be mimicking a more complicated model with a different causal structure. The method of identifying causal direction employed here does rest on a sophisticated version of the *post hoc, ergo propter hoc* principle. The method, however, is not easily fooled. Simple linear structures with reversed causality cannot be constructed to give apparent price-to-factor utilization causality. A more complicated system in which both the quantity of a factor used and its price are endogenous will, except under very special assumptions, yield a bivariate reduced from showing bidirectional causality. The special assumptions required to make endogenous price appear exogenous in a bivariate system must make price essentially identical to a truly exogenous variable. Thus, if price in the sample has been passively and quickly adjusted to match some third variable and if this latter variable is a truly exogenous variable affecting the quantity of a factor used in the production process with a distributed lag, the price might falsely appear to cause the quantity of a factor used. If there is substantial random error, however, in the correspondence between this third variable and price and if that error has a pattern of serial correlation different from that of the third variable, then the bivariate relation between price and factor quantity will appear to show bidirectional causality.

A Methodological Note

In a study such as this, where fairly precise use of F tests is required on groups of coefficients, it is important that the assumption of serially uncorrelated residuals be approximately accurate. A considerable number of approaches have been suggested to guarantee this serial independence. These are not recounted here, but the interested reader is referred to the survey by Pierce and Haugh.[10]

The approach adopted is to select a filter for each of the time series of interest using the method of Box and Jenkins.[11] That is, as Haugh[12] suggests, the regressions between the pair of whitened series

$$X_t^* = F(B)X_t$$

$$(3.2)$$

$$Y_t^* = G(B)Y_t,$$

where $F(B)$ and $G(B)$ are polynomials of the backward shift operator B, are used.

If the filters F(B) and G(B) fail to produce white noise series, substantial positive first-order serial correlation will remain. (The Box–Pierce[13] Q statistic can be used to test for the removal of serial correlation.) Additionally, filtering may produce a perverse effect on approximation error when lag distributions are subject to prior smoothness restrictions. Consequently, no Koyck, Almon, or rational lag restrictions were imposed a priori and the length of the estimated lag was kept reasonably long.

Data

In selecting time series data on factor quantities and prices there are a large number of data sets employing a variety of measurement techniques that could be used. One that has received wide use, and the one employed here, is that developed by Berndt and Wood for four factors of production (capital, labor, energy, and materials) covering the period 1947–1971.

Procedures outlined by Christensen and Jorgenson[14] are used to construct the rental price of capital services from nonresidential structures and producers' durable equipment, taking account of variations in effective tax rates and rates of return, depreciation, and capital gains. Quantity indexes of capital are constructed by divisia aggregation of capital services from nonresidential structures and producers' durable equipment. Finally, the value of capital services is computed as the product of the capital quantity index and the rental price of capital. A more detailed discussion of procedures used in constructing these capital price and quantity indexes is found in Berndt and Christensen.[15]

Since data on labor compensation are readily available, estimates of the price of labor are obtained by first concentrating on the measure of the quantity of labor. The measure of labor services is constructed as a divisia index of production ("blue collar") and nonproduction ("white collar") labor manhours, adjusted for quality changes using the educational attainment indexes of Christensen and Jorgenson. The measure of the value of labor services is total compensation to employees in U.S. manufacturing adjusted for the earnings of proprietors.

The price of labor is then computed as adjusted total labor compensation divided by the quantity of labor services. A more detailed discussion of methodology and data sources used in the construction of the labor price and quantity indexes is presented in the aforementioned paper of Berndt and Christensen.

Annual price and quantity indexes are constructed for energy and other intermediate materials in U.S. manufacturing from 1947 through 1971. Annual interindustry flow tables measuring flows of goods and services from 25 producing sectors to 10 consuming sectors and 5 categories of final demand, in both current and constant dollars, are presented by Faucett Associates.[16] Using these tables, we construct annual Divisia quantity indexes of coal, crude petroleum, refined petroleum products, natural gas, and electrical energy purchased by U.S. manufacturing establishments. The value of energy purchases is then computed as the sum of current dollar purchases of these five energy types. Finally, the price index of energy is formed as the value of total energy purchases divided by the quantity of energy.

Annual quantity indexes of materials are constructed from the Faucett interindustry flow tables as divisia quantity indexes of nonenergy intermediate goods purchased by U.S. manufacturing establishments from agriculture, nonfuel mining, construction, manufacturing excluding petroleum products, transportation, communications, trade, water and sanitary services, and foreign countries (imports). The value of total nonenergy intermediate good purchases is then computed as the sum of current dollar purchases of all these nonenergy intermediate goods. Finally, the price index of materials is formed as the value of total nonenergy intermediate goods purchases divided by the quality of materials.

Filtering

As noted previously, an appropriate filter needs to be used on each of the data series to eliminate the serial correlation problem. A Box–Jenkins model was fit to each of the eight series (four quantity and four price). The results are presented, together with the associated Q statistics, in Table III.2. Due

Table III.2. Data Filters

Series	Model Estimates[a]	Q-Statistic[c]
1. Quantity (X)		
a. Capital	$(1 - B)X_t = (1 + 0.7635B)a_t{}^b$	10.64
b. Labor	$(1 - B)X_t = (1 + 0.2140B)a_t$	8.40
c. Energy	$(1 - B)X_t = (1 + 0.2044B)a_t$	17.55
d. Materials	$(1 - B)X_t = (1 + 0.3123B)a_t$	17.75
2. Price (Y)		
a. Capital	$(1 - B)(1 + 0.0770)Y_t = a_t$	8.41
b. Labor	$(1 - B)(1 - 0.8359)Y_t = a_t$	9.00
c. Energy	$(1 - B)(1 + 0.2825)Y_t = a_t$	3.85
d. Materials	$(1 - B)(1 - 0.3189)Y_t = a_t$	10.48

Notes:

[a] Standard errors of the estimates for Quantity: 0.1037 (Capital) 0.4993 (Labor), 0.4854 (Energy); 0.1438 (Material); for Price: 0.00264 (Capital), 0.3611 (Labor), 0.1191 (Energy), 0.1203 (Material).

[b] a_t is a white-noise series that is identically and independently distributed with mean zero and finite variance.

[c] Based on 20 degrees of freedom.

to the pronounced trends in all of the series, first differencing was required for stationarity. Beyond this, a moving average specification of order 1 effectively flattened the spectral density (removed the serial correlation) of the quantity series, and an autoregressive specification of order 1 did likewise for the price series. The magnitude of each of the Q statistics is such that the null hypothesis of the absence of serial correlation can be accepted at least at the 95 percent level.

One final comment on the effect of filtering is in order before turning to the empirical results. As noted previously, adjustment in the prices of the factors of production to the extent that causality is present will lead to a new optimal level of output. The possibility therefore exists that to the extent that changes in prices precisely emulate the behavior of changes in output, then there will be the inappropriate attribution of causality running from prices to the quantity of the factors of production used whereas the actual direction of causality runs from changing levels of output. Fortunately, for the reason noted earlier in the subsection on a test for directional causality, stringent criteria must be met before the test yields such inaccurate results. Examination of the residuals between output and the various price variables show this not to be the case here.

Directional Causality and the Demand for the Factors of Production

To recapitulate, the causality test will be applied to determine the extent to which the use of factors of production respond to variations in the price of the factors. Economic theory is clear in suggesting that variations in the own price of a factor should initially result in a reduction of the quantity used provided the production function is positive, twice differentiable, and strictly concave. The total effect of such variations on the demand for factors of production, however, is a question that has to be empirically determined.

The summary results of regressions of own price on quantity (i.e., with quantity the dependent variable) for each of the four factors of production considered are presented in Table III.3. As expected, there is a clear indication of directional causality: the regressions are all statistically significant at the 95 percent level or better. Although the actual coefficients as the price terms are not presented (they are quite voluminous and add little insight), their signs are consistent with what we a priori extect, namely, an increase in the price of the factor leads to a reduction in its utilization. The results allow firm acceptance of the null hypothesis that the quantity of a factor used in the production process does respond to variations in its own price.

More important for our considerations here are the impacts on the use of factors of production with regard to changes in the prices of the other factors. A summary of the regression results is given in Tables III.4A through III.4D. The price of capital is statistically significant in influencing the quantity of labor, energy, and materials used in the production process. And, consistently, the price of labor, energy, and materials affects the quantity of capital. Also, though the estimates of the coefficients of the regressions are not given (they are available upon request), they are almost uniformly positive. This

Table III.3. Summary of the Regressions of Own Price on Quantity

		F for Independent Variables [a]	R^2	Degrees of Freedom
1.	Quantity = f(price, 6 past lags)[b]			
	a. Capital	7.73	0.6344	15
	b. Labor	6.99	0.6665	15
	c. Energy	8.02	0.6696	15
	d. Materials	6.59	0.5741	15
2.	Quantity = f(price, 3 future leads 6 past lags)			
	a. Capital	14.34	0.9599	12
	b. Labor	11.98	0.9162	12
	c. Energy	9.64	0.8779	12
	d. Materials	11.04	0.8522	12
3.	Quantity = f(3 future leads)			
	a. Capital	15.05	0.5741	19
	b. Labor	5.76	0.4686	19
	c. Energy	7.65	0.5145	19
	d. Materials	6.07	0.4558	19

Notes:
[a] F − statistic computed from the regression
[b] That is, the regression consists of quantity on a function of price in the current period and price lagged for six previous periods. An analogous interpretation holds for the other specifications in this table as well as for those in Table 3A–Table 3D.

suggests that these factors of production are de facto substitutes and not complements as some empirical studies purport to show. In the time series analysis context here, an increase in the price of capital leads to an increase in the quantity of labor, energy, and materials used. Similarly, an increase in either the price of labor, the price of energy, or the price of materials results in an increase in the quantity of capital used. The results are unambiguous in this regard.

The other price quality interrelationships are also conclusive. The null hypothesis that the price of labor affects the quantity of energy and the quantity of materials used in the production process is rejected, as are the null hypotheses that the price

Table III.4A. Summary of the Regressions of Price of Capital on Quantity

		F for Independent Variables	R^2	Degrees of Freedom
1.	Quantity = f(price, 6 past lags)			
	a. Labor	7.07	0.5175	15
	b. Energy	5.74	0.6272	15
	c. Materials	4.21	0.3493	15
2.	Quantity = f(price, 3 future leads 6 past lags)			
	a. Labor	9.93	0.8371	12
	b. Energy	6.33	0.8450	12
	c. Materials	4.85	0.7106	12
3.	Quantity = f(3 future leads)			
	a. Labor	5.07	0.3122	19
	b. Energy	4.17	0.4389	19
	c. Materials	3.68	0.3545	19

Table III.4B. Summary of the Regressions of Price of Labor on Quantity

		F for Independant Variable	R^2	Degrees of Freedom
1.	Quantity = f(price, 6 past lags)			
	a. Capital	6.12	0.6799	15
	b. Energy	1.02	0.2021	15
	c. Materials	1.41	0.2855	15
2.	Quantity = f(price, 3 future leads, 6 past lags)			
	a. Capital	9.63	0.9525	12
	b. Energy	3.63	0.6523	12
	c. Materials	1.04	0.5822	12
3.	Quantity = f(3 future leads)			
	a. Capital	6.85	0.5639	19
	b. Energy	0.71	0.1596	19
	c. Materials	0.72	0.1190	19

Table III.4C. Summary of the Regressions of Price of Energy on Quantity

	F for Independent Variable	R^2	Degrees of Freedom
1. Quantity = f(price, 6 past lags)			
a. Capital	3.81	0.7919	15
b. Labor	1.07	0.4186	15
c. Materials	1.36	0.4770	15
2. Quantity = f(price, 3 future leads, 6 past lags)			
a. Capital	7.46	0.9762	12
b. Labor	1.11	0.6593	12
c. Materials	1.37	0.6827	12
3. Quantity = f(3 future leads)			
a. Capital	4.45	0.5253	19
b. Labor	0.14	0.0372	19
c. Materials	0.90	0.1948	19

Table III.4D. Summary of the Regressions of Price of Materials on Quantity

	F for Independent Variables	R^2	Degrees of Freedom
1. Quantity = f(price, 6 past lags)			
a. Capital	8.14	0.8907	15
b. Labor	6.37	0.2743	15
c. Energy	1.61	0.5182	15
2. Quantity = f(price, 3 future leads, 6 past lags)			
a. Capital	5.49	0.9680	12
b. Labor	0.34	0.6558	12
c. Energy	0.74	0.6039	12
3. Quantity = f(3 future leads)			
a. Capital	7.52	0.6675	19
b. Labor	2.00	0.3486	19
c. Energy	0.43	0.1023	19

of energy impacts the quantity of labor and the quantity of materials and that the price of materials influences the quantity of labor and the quantity of energy. The results support the contention that not all factors of production are substitutable.

Implications of the Results

The implication of the results obtained in our estimate of production functions is transparent. All factors of production are not substitutable for one another. Consequently, any specification that looks at this potentiality is inappropriate. Thus, a specification such as one of the flexible translog forms that incorporates capital, labor, energy, and materials simultaneously is misguided. (Note that even if the parameter estimates in a translog specification are zero, the partial elasticities of substitution will be, in general, nonzero. As can be seen from the results here, this is not correct.) One must be very judicious in specifying a production function that properly incorporates the realities of substitution.

A second conclusion one can draw from the results is that in the production process there is no support for the contention that the expansion effect outweighs the gross substitution effect. Credence is lent to the notion that any of the factors of production are complementary. Further, in many of the instances of comparing factors pairwise, the production isoquant is characterized as having an invariant marginal rate of technical substitution. That is, a Leontief-type fixed coefficient production function is appropriate.

One caveat should properly be inserted as the closing comment. As noted several times in the foregoing discussion, the nature of the analysis is essentially empirical. The suggested hypotheses are accepted or rejected based on the empirical results of the statistical test for directional causality. The test is well developed and is not a potential delimitor; the data, however, are. To the extent the constructed series are accurate representations of quantities used and prices paid for factors of production, then the results should be aicepted unequivocally. If there are potential weaknesses in any of the series, then the enthusiasm with which the results are accepted should be tempered.

ENERGY SUBSTITUTION

The results of the foregoing section are particularly suggestive as to the substitution relationships between capital, labor, energy, and materials. With the objective of developing an explanatory relationship for total energy consumption in the industrial sector, a model is formulated that is consistent with the empirical results and data availabilities.

Since it was shown that energy is substitutable with capital only, the constant elasticity of substitution (CES)[17] relationship is posited in the form

$$Q = \gamma_e^{\lambda t}[\delta_0 K^{-\zeta} + (1 - \delta_0)E^{-\zeta}]^{v/\zeta}, \qquad (3.3)$$

where Q is total output; E and K are energy and capital inputs, respectively; t denotes the time period; and γ, δ_0, and ζ are parameters. This form of the CES production function imposes Hicks' neutral technical change. (Note that γ is the technological efficiency coefficient, λ is the rate of Hicks' neutral technical changes, and δ_0 and $1 - \delta_0$ are distributional coefficients. The parameter v measures returns to scale so that v equaling 1 implies constant returns to scale.)

Using the standard microeconomic theoretic assumptions,[18] we obtain the result that the marginal product will equal the price of energy. That is,

$$P_E = \frac{\partial Q}{\partial E}P_Q, \qquad (3.4)$$

where P_Q is the price of the output.

Now from relationship (3.3) the marginal product of energy is

$$\frac{\partial Q}{\partial E} = (1 - \delta_0)(\gamma e^{\lambda t})^{-\zeta/v} \frac{Q^{(1+\zeta)/v}}{E^{1+\zeta}}. \qquad (3.5)$$

Substituting relationship (3.5) into relationship (3.4) and rearranging terms, one has:

$$E = v(1 - \delta_0)^{1/(v+\zeta)}(\gamma e^{\lambda t})^{-\zeta/v(1+\zeta)}Q^{(v+\zeta)/v(1+\zeta)}\left[\frac{P_Q}{P_E}\right]^{1/(1+\zeta)}. \qquad (3.6)$$

Taking logarithms and simplifying, the demand for aggregate energy becomes:

$$\log E = C^* - \frac{\lambda[1 - 1/(1 + \zeta)]t}{v}$$

$$+ \frac{(v - 1)/(1 + \zeta) + 1}{v} \log Q + \frac{1}{1 + \zeta} \log \frac{P_Q}{P_E}, \tag{3.7}$$

where C^* is a constant and log denotes Napierian logarithms. The expression $1/(1 + \zeta)$ is the elasticity of substitution between energy and the other factor of production (capital).

The data used to estimate relationship (3.7) came from a variety of sources. Total energy inputs, E, and the price of energy for various two-digit SIC manufacturing industries, P_E, were obtained from the Annual Survey of Manufacturers (ASM) for the period 1947–1978. Data on total output for the various two-digit industries (measured as gross product originating) and the price of output (measured as an index) came from the Bureau of Economic Analysis, U.S. Department of Commerce.

The results of the estimation are given in Table III.5. Since the relationship is nonlinear in the parameters (highly so), a maximum likelihood technique was used. Serial correlation based on the computed Durbin–Watson statistic did not (fortunately) present a problem and hence was not corrected for. The data were pooled across industries utilizing both intra- (i.e., temporal) and interindustry variation.

All of the coefficient estimates are significantly different than zero. An estimate of ζ of -2.7350, implying an elasticity of substitution of -0.5764, confirms the previous conclusion that, with regard to capital and energy, the technology is not characterized by a Leontief fixed coefficient production function. The technique through which this substitution comes about is straightforward. Industrial demand for energy derives from the complex workings of domestic and international economic growth and contraction in addition to changing consumer preferences. At the process level there is little flexibility in the short run for reoptimizing the mix of capital and energy in response to a change in price or availability of either factor.

Table III.5. Aggregate Energy
Demand for the Industrial Sector

Coefficient	Estimate[1]
Constant	4.6097
	(2.2234)
v	0.9361
	(0.3804)
ζ	−2.7350
	(0.9642)
λ	0.0214
	(0.0108)
$\bar{R}^2$	0.8271
D.W. Statistic[2]	1.9674

Notes:
[1] Standard errors of estimates in parentheses
[2] Durbin-Watson Statistic.

Improved process control and plant operation (i.e., house-keeping measures) are generally the first action to be under-taken. These measures de facto constitute movement onto, or very near to, the production-possibility frontier. Over the longer term, switching to alternative fuels and gradual re-placement of depreciated process components with more en-ergy efficient ones will occur. For this longer period, process technologies will change by significant discontinuous magni-tudes as research and development efforts focus on improving energy efficiency.

An equally interesting finding is that the returns to scale parameter v is not significantly different than 1. This implies the presence of constraint returns to scale, which is not sur-prising in light of the fairly large literature showing constant returns to scale in U.S. manufacturing. (See, for example, the survey by Nerlove.[19]) The implication is that the long-run av-erage cost function for production is virtually horizontal. There can be considerable intraindustry variability in this re-sult, but when the aggregation is accomplished specific firm/ industry anomalies disappear.[20]

INTERFUEL SUBSTITUTION

Background

It is important to consider the potential for energy substitution because of the considerable technical flexibility that exists. For example, while some processes in the manufacture of aluminum are energy specific (say, aluminum refining), such is not the case in other processes. Thus, in the fabrication process, distillate and residual fuel oils are substitutes for natural gas. Alternatively, steel produced by the electric arc is substitutable for steel produced by hot iron (with coal being the boiler fuel). Consequently, higher oil prices in the former case and higher coal prices in the latter should result in higher natural gas consumption and electrical energy consumption. Moreover, as the relative prices of the outputs (aluminum and steel) change because of changing relative fuel prices, there will be a change in the fuel mix expenditures.

This is not meant to imply that all fuels are uniformly substitutable. For example, bituminous coal in the production of iron cannot be replaced by electrical energy. Nor can natural gas be replaced as a feedstock in the processing of anhydrous ammonia by coal or oil. Energy is not substitutable in all instances.

The nature and extent of interfuel substitution possibilities in manufacturing are basic to the question of reducing dependency on imported oil.

The characteristics of energy demand can be expected to differ across industries, reflecting the different technologies involved. Differences in energy consumption across industries are due both to differences in output and to differences in the energy intensiveness of production. The apparent differences in energy consumption across industries indicate that the interrelationships between demands for each type of energy should be examined on an industry-by-industry basis.[21]

Although there have been several econometric studies of manufacturing, little attention has been paid to the demand for individual energy components in the United States. Previous studies have generally aggregated all types of energy into a single input and, therefore, have not provided information on the elasticities of demand and substitution for each type of energy.[22]

The approach for the estimation of substitution relationships that has been capturing the most attention recently is the transcendental logarithmic price-possibility frontier, or—more simply—the translog price-possibility frontier. The price-possibility frontier is a transcendental function of the logarithms of the price of inputs. The translog price-possibility frontier was introduced by Christensen and associates.[23] It distinguishes itself from earlier approaches in that it begins by positing, as an analog to the production-possibility frontier, a price-possibility frontier of a general neoclassical specification. In conjunction with assumptions of perfect competition, factor input equations are derived which must be estimated simultaneously to allow for the theoretically imposed restrictions on the parameters. The approach offers distinct advantages over other approaches in that an explicit theoretical model serves as the basis for specification and reduces the problem of multicollinearity by decreasing the number of parameters to be estimated.

Extensive use of this approach was made by Jorgenson and Berndt in Chapter 3 of *Energy Resources and Economic Growth*.[24] An energy submodel for the manufacturing sector of a translog price-possibility frontier along the lines of Jorgenson and Berndt will be developed in the next section. Subsequent to that, the model will be empirically implemented and the implications of the results assessed.

A Price Possibility Frontier for Fuel Inputs

Following Jorgenson and Berndt, it is hypothesized that there exists a twice-differentiable production frontier relating the output of manufacturing (Q) to the inputs of capital (K), labor (L), and energy inputs (coal, X_C; oil, X_O; natural gas, X_G; and electrical energy, X_{EE}). Further constant returns to scale and Hicks' neutral technical change are assumed. Corresponding to this production possibility frontier is a price-possibility frontier specified as

$$P = \Omega(P_K, P_L, P_C, P_O, P_G, P_{EE}), \tag{3.8}$$

where P_K, P_L, P_C, P_O, P_G, and P_{EE} denote the input price of capital, labor, coal, oil, natural gas, and electrical energy, respectively, and P is the price of manufacturing output.

Next it is assumed that coal, oil, natural gas, and electrical energy constitute a separable and homogeneous energy aggregate, E, allowing one to reformulate relationship (3.8) as

$$P = \Omega[P_K, P_L, \Omega_E(P_C, P_O, P_G, P_{EE})] \tag{3.9}$$

$$= \Omega(P_K, P_L, P_E)$$

and

$$P_E = \Omega_E(P_C, P_O, P_G, P_{EE}). \tag{3.10}$$

Thus, Ω is stated as two separate submodels—one in which capital, labor, and aggregate energy inputs are determined, and a second in which specific energy inputs are determined. It should be noted that relationship (3.10) influences the aggregate energy input choice directly through P_E in relationship (3.9).

The sufficient conditions for this specification are important.[25] Separability requires that the ratio of the cost shares of any two energy inputs be independent of the prices outside the aggregate energy input such as capital and labor. De facto, the ratio of the shares depends just on fuel prices. Linear homogeneity in input prices in relationships (3.9) and (3.10), in turn, implies that the cost shares of fuels are independent of total expenditures on the energy inputs. Jorgenson and Berndt use this assumption to permit the estimation of relationships (3.9) and (3.10) separately and consequently conserve degrees of freedom. In the present instance, this assumption is made to allow the estimation of Ω_E.

It is desirable to specify a general functional form which has a minimal number of a priori restrictions. The translog price-possibility frontier allows a large degree of generality since it places no restrictions on the Allen partial elasticities of substitution and can be viewed as a second-order approximation to any arbitrary twice-differentiable price-possibility frontier.

The translog price-possibility frontier of the energy submodel can be expressed as

$$\log P_E = \alpha_o + \sum_i \alpha_i \log P_i$$

$$+ \tfrac{1}{2} \sum_i \sum_j \gamma_{ij} \log P_i \log P_j \qquad (i, j = C, O, G, EE), \quad (3.11)$$

where $\gamma_{ij} = \gamma_{ji}$; P_E is the price of energy; the P_i's are the prices of the energy inputs; and the α's and γ's are unknown parameters.

In order to correspond to a well-behaved production function, a price-possibility frontier must be homogeneous of degree 1 in prices. That is, for a fixed level of output, total energy expenditures must increase proportionately when all energy prices increase proportionately. This implies the following relationships among the parameters:

$$\sum_i \alpha_i = 1 \tag{3.12}$$

and

$$\sum_i \gamma_{ij} = 0 \qquad (i, j = C, O, G, EE). \tag{3.13}$$

A convenient feature of the price-possibility frontier approach is that the derived demand functions for the energy inputs can be easily computed by partially differentiating relationship (3.11) with respect to the energy prices, i.e.,

$$\frac{\partial P_E}{\partial P_i} = X_i. \tag{3.14}$$

This result, known as Shephard's lemma,[26] is conveniently expressed in logarithmic form for the translog price possibility frontier as

$$\frac{\partial \log P_E}{\partial \log P_i} = \frac{P_i X_i}{\sum_j P_j X_j} = S_i \qquad (i, j = C, O, G, EE), \tag{3.15}$$

where S_i indicates the cost share of the ith energy input. The translog price-possibility frontier yields the cost share equations as follows:

$$S_C = \alpha_C + \gamma_{CC} \log P_C + \gamma_{CO} \log P_O$$

$$+ \gamma_{CG} \log P_G + \gamma_{CEE} \log P_{EE}, \tag{3.16a}$$

$$S_O = \alpha_O + \gamma_{OC} \log P_C + \gamma_{OO} \log P_O$$
$$+ \gamma_{OG} \log P_G + \gamma_{OEE} \log P_{EE}, \tag{3.16b}$$

$$S_G = \alpha_G + \gamma_{GC} \log P_C + \gamma_{GO} \log P_O$$
$$+ \gamma_{GG} \log P_G + \gamma_{GEE} \log P_{EE}, \tag{3.16c}$$

$$S_{EE} = \alpha_{EE} + \gamma_{EEC} \log P_C + \gamma_{EEO} \log P_O$$
$$+ \gamma_{EEG} \log P_G + \gamma_{EEEE} \log P_{EE}. \tag{3.16d}$$

The cost shares sum to unity.

The application of Shephard's lemma implies that energy prices are exogenously determined from the industrial sector. Consequently, actual energy prices can be used in the estimation process without introducing the concern over simultaneous equation bias. The markets for coal, oil, natural gas, and electrical energy are national and international. As a result, a specific industry will have minimal discernible impact on the delivered energy price.

Uzawa[27] has shown that Allen's[28] partial elasticities of substitution between energy inputs are given by

$$\sigma_{ij} = \frac{\Omega_E \cdot \Omega_E^{ij}}{\Omega_E^i \cdot \Omega_E^j}, \tag{3.17}$$

where the superscripts on Ω_E indicate the partial differentiation of the energy submodel (3.10) with respect to the energy prices. For the translog price-possibility frontier, we have

$$\sigma_{ii} = \frac{\gamma_{ii} + S_i^2 - S_i}{S_i^2} \tag{3.18a}$$

$$\sigma_{ij} = \frac{\gamma_{ij} + S_i S_j}{S_i S_j} \quad (i \neq j) \quad \text{for } i, j = C, O, G, EE. \tag{3.18b}$$

Further, Allen has shown that the elasticities of substitution are related to the price elasticities of demand for the energy inputs, η_{ij}, as

$$\eta_{ij} = S_j \sigma_{ij}. \tag{3.19}$$

This formulation assumes that $\Sigma_j \, \eta_{ij} = 0$.

The partial elasticities of substitution are invariant with regard to the ordering of the energy input factors. Therefore, $\sigma_{ij} = \sigma_{ji}$, although in general $\eta_{ij} \neq \eta_{ji}$.

Estimation Procedure

It is feasible to estimate the parameters of the price possibility frontier using ordinary least squares analysis. This technique is certainly attractive from the point of view of simplicity. However, it neglects the additional information contained in the share equations (3.16a) through (3.16d), which are also easily estimable. Furthermore, even for a modest number of factor prices, the translog price-possibility frontier has a large number of regressors which do not vary greatly across industries. Hence multicollinearity may be a problem, resulting in imprecise parameter estimates.

An alternative estimation procedure, and the approach used here, is to estimate jointly the cost-share equations as a multivariate regression system. This procedure is satisfactory since the cost-share equations include all the parameters of the price-possibility frontier except the constant and no information is lost by not including the price-possibility frontier in the estimation procedure.

Additive disturbances are specified for each of the share equations. Since the cost-share equations are derived by differentiation, they do not contain the disturbance term from the cost function. It is assumed that the disturbances have a joint normal distribution. Following Zellner,[29] nonzero correlations across industries are allowed but zero correlations across time are imposed. However, his proposed estimation procedure is not operational for the current model. The estimated disturbance covariance matrix required to implement Zellner's procedure is singular because the disturbances on the share equations must sum to zero for each region. The Zellner procedure can be made operational by deleting one of the share equations from the system. However, the estimates so obtained will not be invariant with regard to which equation is deleted.

Barten[30] has shown that maximum likelihood estimates of a system of share equations with one equation deleted are invariant no matter which equation is dropped. Kmenta and Gilbert[31] have shown that iteration of the Zellner estimation procedure until convergence results in maximum likelihood estimates. Iterating the Zellner procedure is a computationally efficient method for obtaining maximum likelihood estimates and is the procedure which is employed here.

Data

The share equations are estimated with pooled annual data on energy prices and quantities consumed compiled from the Annual Survey of Manufacturers for 1958 through 1978. Interindustry coefficients are not included in the estimating equations because the estimation procedure captures such variation through the variance–covariance matrix.

Empirical Results

The maximum likelihood estimates are invariant with regard to which equation is omitted. Consequently, Eqs. (3.16a) through (3.16c) were estimated and the coefficient estimates of Eq. (3.16d) were derived from these. Linear homogeneity in fuel-price constraints have been imposed. Additional regularity conditions which the price-possibility frontier must satisfy in order to correspond to well-behaved production structures are monotonicity and convexity in fuel prices. To fulfill these conditions, positive fitted cost shares and negative definiteness of the bordered Hessian matrix of the price-possibility frontier are required. These conditions are generally met; hence it is concluded that the estimated price-possibility frontier represents a well-behaved production structure. Serial correlation, as with most time series models, has proved to be a problem. Consequently, it has been corrected for in each of the estimated share equations.

One additional issue presents itself: Are the parameters on the share equations symmetric? That is, does $\gamma_{ij} = \gamma_{ji}$? To test for symmetry, which implies that an increase in the price of energy input j will affect the expenditure share on energy input i to the same extent as a rise in the price of energy input i affects the expenditure on energy input, a Quandt test is employed. The test consists of the following steps:

Denote the determinants of the unrestricted and restricted estimates of the disturbance covariance matrix by $|\hat{\Sigma}_u|$ and $|\hat{\Sigma}_r|$ when equations (3.16a) through (3.16c) are estimated. The likelihood ratio becomes

$$\beta = \left(\frac{|\hat{\Sigma}_u|}{|\hat{\Sigma}_r|}\right)^{-T/2}, \tag{3.20}$$

where T is the number of observations. The hypothesis is tested using the fact that $-2 \log \beta$ has a chi-square distribution with degrees of freedom equal to the number of independent restrictions being imposed.[32] The test was performed with the null hypothesis being that symmetry holds. The determinant of the unconstrained covariance matrix was 2458.70 while the determinant of the constrained covariance matrix was 2456.71, indicating that the null hypothesis cannot be rejected at the 95 percent level.

Moreover, a preliminary examination of the results suggested that the serial correlation coefficient was equal across share equations. This constraint was imposed and the Quandt test employed. Assuming that symmetry is valid, the serial correlation constrained determinant was 2454.89, suggesting that the effect of serial correlation is the same across share equations.

As a result of these two tests, the reported empirical estimates impose the symmetry constraint and equality of serial correlation constraint across share equations.

The set of parameter estimates is given in Table III.6. Most of the estimates are significantly different than zero at the 95 percent level, leading to the conclusion that price elasticities and elasticities of substitution are not zero.

Estimates of the average two-digit SIC price elasticities of demand over the period 1958–1978 are presented in Table III.7. (Estimates of the elasticities of substitution are not reported since they provide little additional insight.) Own-price elasticities should be negative and cross-price elasticities should be positive. This is precisely the pattern that evolves.

One sees a fairly sizeable range in industry price elasticities of demand in Table III.7. The differences are attributable entirely to the energy input share composition. For example, SIC 27 (printing and publishing), with the highest expenditure share of electrical energy in 1978 (78 percent), has the most inelastic demand for electrical energy (-0.14); on the other hand, SIC 32 (stone, clay and glass products), with a cost share of 29 percent, has a price elasticity of -0.49. These results follow from the properties of Eqs. (3.18a), (3.18b), and (3.19) and the negative estimated coefficients for γ_{CC}, γ_{OO}, γ_{GG}, and γ_{EEEE}.

Table III.6. Parameter Estimates for
the Translog Energy Model[1]

Parameter	Estimates
α_C	−0.0437 (0.0214)
α_O	0.5806 (0.1603)
α_G	0.1216 (0.0549)
α_{EE}	0.4977 (0.0409)
γ_{CC}	−0.0998 (0.0105)
γ_{CO}	0.0220 (0.0098)
γ_{CG}	0.0067 (0.0012)
γ_{CEE}	0.0711 (0.0069)
γ_{OO}	−0.0510 (0.0246)
γ_{OG}	0.0118 (0.0050)
γ_{OE}	0.0172 (0.0074)
γ_{GG}	−0.0950 (0.0105)
γ_{GEE}	0.0765 (0.0075)
γ_{EEEE}	−0.1648 (0.0132)
ρ^2	0.9199 (0.1127)

Notes:
[1] Standard error of estimates in parenthesis.
[2] Serial correlation coefficient.

Table III.7 Estimates of Two-Digit Industry Price Elasticities, 1958–1978

Industry	η_{CC}	η_{OO}	η_{GG}	η_{EEEE}	η_{CO}	η_{CG}	η_{CE}	η_{OC}	η_{OG}	η_{OE}	η_{GC}	η_{GO}	η_{GE}	η_{EEC}	η_{EEO}	η_{EEG}
1. SIC 20	−0.95	−0.13	−0.34	−0.36	0.10	0.13	0.31	0.10	0.11	0.03	0.17	0.14	0.04	0.89	0.07	0.10
2. SIC 21	−0.80	−0.02	−0.39	−0.35	0.07	0.17	0.40	0.04	0.03	0.02	0.05	0.12	0.07	0.79	0.07	0.05
3. SIC 22	−0.93	−0.02	−0.36	−0.28	0.18	0.08	0.29	0.11	0.02	0.04	0.03	0.01	0.04	0.63	0.18	0.04
4. SIC 23	−1.09	−0.12	−0.48	−0.23	0.17	0.01	0.20	0.27	0.14	0.06	0.01	0.01	0.04	0.36	0.30	0.05
5. SIC 24	−1.22	−0.31	−0.20	−0.35	0.06	0.01	0.20	0.33	0.19	0.19	0.01	0.05	0.06	0.56	0.33	0.04
6. SIC 25	−0.93	−0.48	−0.03	−0.26	0.36	0.11	0.28	0.17	0.03	0.01	0.06	0.04	0.01	0.17	0.08	0.10
7. SIC 26	−0.72	−0.21	−0.21	−0.48	0.11	0.11	0.56	0.06	0.11	0.01	0.12	0.09	0.09	0.56	0.01	0.19
8. SIC 27	−1.70	−0.49	−0.04	−0.14	0.62	0.51	0.12	0.55	0.02	0.06	0.21	0.06	0.01	0.39	0.05	0.09
9. SIC 28	−0.90	−0.69	−0.29	−0.33	0.42	0.42	0.33	0.15	0.05	0.04	0.14	0.01	0.04	0.52	0.28	0.12
10. SIC 29	−1.63	−0.30	−1.04	−0.48	0.04	0.04	0.24	0.87	0.02	0.44	0.20	0.01	0.21	0.71	0.23	0.36
11. SIC 30	−0.93	−0.04	−0.32	−0.25	0.16	0.16	0.27	0.11	0.04	0.03	0.03	0.02	0.53	0.18	0.15	0.04
12. SIC 31	−0.87	−0.16	−0.33	−0.33	0.06	0.06	0.32	0.06	0.02	0.07	0.04	0.01	0.06	0.43	0.21	0.05
13. SIC 32	−1.05	−0.11	−0.37	−0.49	0.16	0.16	0.44	0.08	0.08	0.08	0.34	0.28	0.10	0.41	0.22	0.09
14. SIC 33	−1.28	−0.25	−0.10	−0.34	0.08	0.11	0.25	0.12	0.12	0.11	0.06	0.06	0.02	0.14	0.26	0.08
15. SIC 34	−1.05	−0.09	−0.34	−0.31	0.23	0.23	0.17	0.09	0.09	0.05	0.10	0.10	0.08	0.65	0.18	0.21
16. SIC 35	−1.09	−0.02	−0.17	−0.28	0.22	0.23	0.23	0.04	0.04	0.03	0.08	0.04	0.01	0.22	0.16	0.06
17. SIC 36	−1.00	−0.31	−0.18	−0.24	0.37	0.37	0.21	0.10	0.01	0.01	0.07	0.01	0.24	0.36	0.03	0.11
18. SIC 37	−0.91	−0.27	−0.06	−0.25	0.32	0.31	0.23	0.04	0.04	0.06	0.07	0.02	0.01	0.16	0.04	0.01
19. SIC 38	−0.92	−0.08	−0.05	−0.34	0.10	0.16	0.33	0.05	0.07	0.04	0.08	0.04	0.01	0.40	0.13	0.13
20. SIC 39	−1.20	−0.12	−0.03	−0.25	0.20	0.20	0.18	0.06	0.05	0.07	0.01	0.04	0.06	0.44	0.29	0.24
Total U.S. Manufacturing	−1.07	−0.27	−0.33	−0.39	0.18	0.17	0.29	0.13	0.06	0.05	0.12	0.07	0.05	0.41	0.24	0.13

We see that the industrial sector is responding to relative price changes, though the response is not equal in both directions. This arises primarily because of differences in the technology involved in changeover of existing plants from one fuel to another. Coal, oil, natural gas, and electrical energy are all substantially in competition with each other as energy sources (in most industries), and every indication from the results point to the fact that industries are responsive to relative price changes when making their energy choice.

How is the observed interfuel substitution accomplished? First, specific boilers may be able to utilize more than one type of fuel. While natural gas may be the preferred fuel, for example, because of its cleanliness, many boilers are dual fired (using both oil and natural gas), allowing for increased use of oil as the relative prices change. Changing relative energy prices alter the relative marginal costs of operating various types of equipment using different energy sources and hence provide an incentive to switch to the lower-cost energy by either retrofitting or replacing the existing equipment stock. Moreover, those investing in new equipment will opt for the lowest-cost energy source, thus giving an overall appearance of substitution in the guise of relative expenditure shifts.

Next, the recent dramatic escalation in the price of energy has provided a considerable incentive to conserve. Obvious housekeeping measures such as conducting preventive maintenance (plugging leaks), expansion of waste heat recovery, and reducing heat loads to the maximum extent possible are thus being more actively pursued.

Finally, changing fuel prices relative to the price of energy-using equipment provide an incentive to replace the existing capital stock with a more efficient stock. The rapidity with which this can occur depends upon the size of the change in the cost of the factors of production (i.e., energy relative to capital) and the ability of individual industries to take advantage of new, more energy-efficient technologies.[33]

The estimates presented in Table III.7 provide a basis for the calculation of average elasticities across all industries. Long-run own-price elasticities for the aggregate U.S. industrial sector are -1.07, -0.27, -0.33, and -0.39 for coal, oil, natural gas, and electrical energy, respectively. These are comparable to the price elasticity estimates for the industrial sector found by Griffin for 20 countries in the world.[34] The elasticities obtained here, however, are somewhat smaller than those estimated by Halvorsen[35] who computed cross-sectional estimates for two-digit SIC industries across states for 1971. He finds own-price elasticities of -1.46, -2.75, -1.32, and -0.66 for coal, oil, natural gas, and electrical energy, respectively. These results are problematic when we consider that cross-sectional estimates typically bias the response downward because capital stock efficiency improvements are not reflected. The results of Norman and Russell[36] are somewhat more consistent with those given here. Using two-digit SIC (cross-sectional) data for the period 1954–1971, they find average elasticities for all fuels to be about -0.48 and for electrical energy to be about -0.40.

Time series analyses, in particular, have shown that oil demand is very inelastic. For example, Hudson and Jorgenson,[37] applying the translog approach to the energy subsector of the manufacturing industry, report price elasticities for 1969 of 0.00, -0.08, -0.04, and -0.06 for coal, oil, natural gas, and electrical energy, respectively. Comparison of the results derived here and those of Hudson and Jorgenson is particularly interesting since it tends to confirm the suspicion that the earlier, pure-time series approach captured only a portion of the long-run price response in industries involving long periods for capital turnover.

As previously observed, a nice theoretical property of the translog formulation is that the sum of own- and cross-price elasticities among fuels is zero. It is instructive to consider the magnitude of the cross-price elasticities in order to determine the main channels of interfuel substitution. Table III.7 shows these elasticities. The effect of higher oil prices, say, will create a significant stimulus to natural gas and electrical energy consumption. Therefore, the alternative sources to oil will be natural gas and electrical energy. Thus, in light of the severe availability problem of natural gas to industrial consumers in particular, future oil price increases do not bode well for the industrial sector.

The study by Hudson and Jorgenson of the industrial sector provides a basis for comparison of cross-price elasticities as well. Based on 1969 estimates, they find the elasticity of the demand for coal with respect to the price of gas to be 0.12 while the elasticity of demand for coal with respect to the price of oil (distillate and residual) is 0.06. The elasticity of demand for electrical energy with respect to the price of gas is 0.09. The elasticity of demand for coal with respect to the price of gas is −0.10, indicating complementarity. While the standard errors of their estimates are not given, it seems unrealistic to assume that the latter result is statistically significant. In all cases, the results obtained here suggest comparatively greater energy substitution effects.

Two points should be noted with respect to the interpretation of the estimated elasticities. First, the estimates reflect long-run effects of prices on energy demand. Short-run effects can be expected to be considerably smaller. Second, the elasticities do not measure the net effects of price change on consumption of oil, natural gas, and coal. Because these fuels are inputs in the production of electrical energy, the net effects of price changes will include changes in the demand for fuels in electric power generation.[38]

Policy Implications

These results indicate that relative changes in fuel prices have significant effects on fossil fuel consumption. This, in turn, has important implications for public policy. In particular, the market system appears better able to deal with exogenous shifts in energy supplies than has frequently been assumed in the formulation of public policies with respect to the energy crisis.

An important question, however, in regard to public policy, has been whether this market response is of sufficient magnitude to mitigate the need for legislation explicitly prohibiting the use of some energy sources (the alternative being the imposition of an energy-specific use tax on oil or natural gas). Unfortunately, the responsiveness of the industrial sector to relative price changes was not considered when the Powerplant and Industrial Fuel Use Act (PIFUA) was passed in 1978. Essentially this act prohibits new plants from using oil or natural gas as primary fuel sources (unless exempted), and existing facilities cannot burn natural gas after January 1, 1990 (unless exempted). [These issues are more fully discussed in the *Annual Report to Congress* (1980) of the U.S. Department of Energy.[39] As is characteristic of the decision-making process preceding many government regulations, the market mechanism was relegated to the background. That need not have been the case. Appropriate incentives (or penalties) could have been offered to lessen the dependence on foreign crude and to divert natural gas to other uses. The one thing that PIFUA does that the econometric results here suggest would not necessarily occur is the complete elimination of the use of natural gas as a boiler fuel.

Another limitation on the free working of the market has been the restriction of coal supplies by federal government coal-leasing policies. The U.S. Department of the Interior stopped most leasing of federal coal reserves in 1971. The moratorium was made official in 1973. The Interior Department has estimated that 200 billion tons of coal production could be made available if all federal coal reserves in the western United States were opened for leasing. Continuation of the coal leasing moratorium will reduce the available coal resource base and consequently raise the price of coal to electric utilities. This moratorium in conjunction with PIFUA is expected to significantly impact the price of electrical energy to the final consumer. Its relaxation would lead to a slight reduction in the price of coal which, from the results presented in the preceding section, would provide an incentive to switch to coal without the government intervention manifest in PIFUA.

TESTING FOR MODEL STABILITY

Major attention has focused on the demand for energy in the industrial sector. Of significant concern in the context of drawing meaningful inferences from the historical period as well as over any forecast horizon is whether the observed relationships (i.e., price elasticities) are stable. (Stability is defined in the statistical sense of the estimated coefficients of the explanatory variables remaining constant over time.) Policy inferences are made on the basis of past behavior. If the functional relationship has been subject to change, then necessarily the inferences will be, at least in part, unsatisfactory.

The purpose of this section is to examine the question of the existence of a stable demand for energy inputs utilizing a statistical test developed by Brown et al.[40] The approach is adopted in deference to others available (e.g., the Chow test[41]) because it does not require prior knowledge of the shifts but rather tests for the presence of such occurrences over the sample period.

To give an appreciation of the aforementioned test, it is briefly discussed below. A way of investigating the time variation of a regression coefficient is to fit the regression on a short segment of n successive observations and to move this segment along the series. A significance test for constancy based on this approach is derived from the results of regressions based on nonoverlapping time segments. The method relies on a test statistic which equals the difference between the sum of squared residuals of the entire sample less the cumulative sum of squared residuals of the nonoverlapping segments divided by the cumulative sum of squared residuals of the nonoverlapping segments. The null hypothesis that the regression relationship is constant over time implies that the value of the test statistic is distributed as F. Specifically, consider the time segments for a moving regression of length $n - (1, n)$, $[(n + 1), (2n)]$, ..., $[(p - 1)n + 1, T]$, where p is the integral part of T/n and the variance ratio considered (i.e., the homogeneity statistic) is

$$\omega = \frac{(T - kp)}{(kp - k)} \frac{S(1, T) - \Delta}{\Delta}, \qquad (3.21)$$

where k is the number of regressions; $\Delta = \{S(1, n) + [S(n + 1), 2n] + \cdots + [(pn - n + 1), T]\}$; and $S(r, s)$ is the residual sum of squares from the regression calculated from observations $t = r$ to s inclusive. This is equivalent to the usual "between groups over within groups" ratio of mean squares and under H_0 is distributed as $F(kp - k, T - kp)$.

In light of the previous discussion, the objective is to explicitly test for the stability of the demand for energy in the industrial sector over the period 1958–1978. Dividing the data into equal length intervals (i.e., $p = 20$, $n = 21$) allows for the computation of the test statistic for each of the share equations. What is done is equivalent to pooling across all 20 two-

Table III.8. Computed Value of the Test Statistic ω

Share Equation	Computed Value of ω	Tabulated Critical Value[1]
1. Coal	0.8641	1.39
2. Oil	0.9227	1.39
3. Natural Gas	1.1760	1.39

Note:
[1] That is $F_{0.05}$ (95,320)

digit SIC industries for a given year and then examining the stability across years. As noted, one of the equations must be deleted and as before the electrical energy equation is selected.

The computed value of ω via Eq. (3.21), the test statistic, for the three share equations is given in Table III.8. The results are conclusive. None of the equations for the demand for energy are unstable over the period 1958–1978.

The implications of the results are transparent for estimating the demand for energy by consumers in the industrial sector. Events over the past two and one-half decades have left unchanged the demand for coal, oil, and natural gas (and implicitly the demand for electrical energy). That is, for the energy inputs, the relative importance of the price of coal, oil, natural gas, and electrical energy in influencing the expenditure shares has remained stable.

Caution, however, must be exercised in inferring that the quantity demanded of coal, oil, natural gas, and electrical energy has not changed. The results of the estimation in the foregoing section show that the prices of all energy sources influence each expenditure share. Consequently, an increase in the price of electrical energy will lead to an increase in the quantity of natural gas consumed. The magnitude of this response, however, over the period 1958–1978 did not vary. That is, the share elasticities for the various forms of energy did not change.

CONCLUSION

The importance of energy as a factor of production is not particularly well understood. As a result, a test for directional causality is used to investigate whether there is any identifiable relationship between variations in energy prices and the utilization of other factors. Based on the results that suggest that energy price affects capital use, a constant elasticity of substitution production function is hypothesized and employed as the vehicle to get a specification for the total demand for energy in the industrial sector. The empirical results confirm the substitution possibilities between energy and capital. The price responses consist of adaptation as well as capital stock turnover.

Interfuel substitution, a priori, seem to be of considerable magnitude. Consequently, an appropriate model is developed and estimated. All energy sources are demonstrated to be substitutable. Coal is the most price responsive, with the other three being of approximately equal size. The results are not inconsistent with other studies of energy substitution. Several ways of realizing this interfuel substitution are suggested, including retrofitting existing equipment and accelerated capital stock turnover, hence more rapidly taking advantage of technological improvements in energy efficiency.

Finally, the issue of stability of the demand for specific energy types is considered. Utilizing a test proposed by Brown, Durbin, and Evans, we find that the demands for coal, oil, natural gas, and electrical energy have remained stable over the past two and one-half decades.

NOTES AND REFERENCES

1. M. Fuss and D. McFadden, *Production Functions: A Dual Approach.* Amsterdam: North-Holland Publishing Co., 1979.
2. N.D. Uri, "Industrial Energy Efficiency: A Look at the Data." *Socio-Economic Planning Sciences 14:*251–256, 1980.
3. W.H. Branson, *Macroeconomic Theory and Policy,* (2nd ed.). New York: Harper and Row Publishers, 1979.
4. E.R. Berndt and D.O. Wood, "Technology, Prices, and the Derived Demand for Energy." *Review of Economics and Statistics 57*(August): 259–268, 1975; and E.R. Berndt and D.O. Wood, "Engineering and Economic Interpretation of Energy–Capital Complementarity." *American Economic Review 69:*342–354, 1979.
5. J. Henderson and R.E. Quandt, *Microeconomic Theory* (2nd ed.). New York: McGraw-Hill Book Company, 1971.
6. L. Johansen, *Production Functions.* Amsterdam: North-Holland Publishing Company, 1972.

7. C.W.J. Granger, "Investigating Causal Relations by Econometric Models and Cross Spectral Methods." *Econometrica 37:*424–438, 1967.

8. C.A. Sims, "Money, Income, and Causality." *American Economic Review 62:*540–552, 1972.

9. J.M. Price, "The Characterization of Instantaneous Causality." *Journal of Econometrics 10:*253–256, 1979.

10. D.A. Pierce and L.D. Haugh, "Causality in Temporal Systems: Characterization and a Survey." *Journal of Econometrics 5:*265–293, 1977.

11. G.E.P. Box and G.M. Jenkins, *Time Series Analysis.* San Francisco: Holden-Day, Inc., 1971.

12. L.D. Haugh, "Checking the Independence of Two Covariance-Stationary Time Series: A Univariate Residual Cross Correlation Approach." *Journal of the American Statistical Association 71:*378–385, 1976.

13. G.E.P. Box and D.A. Pierce, "Distribution of Residual Autocorrelations in Autoregressive-Integrated Moving Average Time Series Models." *Journal of the American Statistical Association 65:*219–229, 1970.

14. L.R. Christensen and D.W. Jorgenson, "The Measurement of U.S. Real Capital Input 1929–1967." *Review of Income and Wealth,* pp. 293–320, 1969.

15. E.R. Berndt and L.R. Christensen, "The Translog Function and the Substitution of Equipment, Structures, and Labor in U.S. Manufacturing, 1929–1968." *Journal of Econometrics,* pp. 81–114, 1973.

16. Faucett Associates, "Data Development for the I–O Energy Model." Chevy Chase, Md.: Jack Faucett Associates, 1973.

17. K.J. Arrow, H.B. Chenery, B.S. Minhan, R.M. Solow, "Capital-Labor Substitution and Economic Efficiency." *The Review of Economics and Statistics 41:*225–250, 1960.

18. J.P. Gould and C.E. Ferguson, *Microeconomic Theory,* (6th ed.). Homewood, Ill.: R.D. Irwin, 1981.

19. M. Nerlove, *Identification and Estimation of Cobb-Douglas Production Functions.* Chicago: Rand-McNally and Company, 1968.

20. Y. Grunfeld and Z. Griliches, "Is Aggregation Necessarily Bad?" *The Review of Economics and Statistics 42:*1–13, 1960.

21. The Conference Board, *Energy Consumption in Manufacturing.* Cambridge, Mass.: Ballinger Publishing Co., 1974.

22. See, for example, the surveys contained in A. Faruqui, *Industrial Energy Substitution in a Vintage Model of Production,* Electric Power Research Institute, Palo Alto 1980; R. Halvorsen, *Econometric Models of U.S. Energy Demand,* D.C. Heath and Co., Lexington, 1978.

23. L.R. Christensen, D.W. Jorgenson, and L.J. Lau, "Transcendental Logarithmic Production Frontiers." *The Review of Economics and Statistics 55*(February):28–45, 1973.

24. D.W. Jorgenson and E.R. Berndt, "Production Structure," in *Energy Resources and Economic Growth,* D.W. Jorgenson and H.S. Houthakker (eds.). Lexington, Mass.: Data Resources Incorporated, 1973.

25. E.R. Berndt and L.R. Christensen, "The Internal Structure of Functional Relationships: Separability, Substitution and Aggregation." *Review of Economic Studies 40*(July):403–410, 1973.

26. R.W. Shepard, *Cost and Production Functions.* Princeton, N.J.: Princeton University Press, 1953.

27. H. Uzawa, "Production Functions with Constant Elasticities of Substitution." *The Review of Economics and Statistics 44*(October):291–299, 1962.

28. R.G.D. Allen, *Mathematical Analysis for Economists.* London: MacMillan and Company, 1938.

29. A. Zellner, "An Efficient Method of Estimating Seemingly Unrelated Regressions and Tests for Aggregation Bias." *Journal of the American Statistical Association 57*(June):348–368, 1962.

30. A.P. Barten, "Maximum Likelihood Estimation of a Complete System of Demand Equations." *European Economic Review 1*(Fall):7–73, 1969.

31. J. Kmenta and R.F. Gilbert, "Small Sample Properties of Alternative Estimators of Seemingly Unrelated Regressions." *Journal of the American Statistical Association 63*(December):1180–1200, 1968.

32. S. Goldfeld and R.E. Quandt, *Nonlinear Methods in Econometrics.* Amsterdam: North-Holland Publishing Company, 1972.

33. H.S. Leff, R.S. Mack and J.F. Bodine, *Potential for Future Energy Conservation.* Oak Ridge, Tenn.: Institute for Energy Analysis, 1980.

34. J.M. Griffin, *Energy Conservation in the OECD: 1980 to 2000.* Cambridge, Mass.: Ballinger Publishing Company, 1979.

35. R. Halvorsen, *Econometric Models of U.S. Energy Demand.* Lexington, Mass.: D.C. Heath and Company, 1978.

36. M.R. Norman and R.R. Russell, *Development of Methods for Forecasting the National Industrial Demand for Energy.* Palo Alto, Calif.: Electric Power Research Institute, 1976.

37. E.A. Hudson and D.W. Jorgenson, "U.S. Energy Policy and Economic Growth, 1975–2000." *Bell Journal of Economics and Management Science 5:*461–514, 1974.

38. N.D. Uri, "Regional Forecasting of the Demand for Fossil Fuels by Electric Utilities." *Regional Science and Urban Economics 11:*87–100, 1981.

39. U.S. Department of Energy, *Annual Report to Congress,* Volume 3. Washington, D.C.: U.S. Government Printing Office, 1980, p. 332–333.

40. R.L. Brown, J. Durbin and J.M. Evans, "Techniques for Testing the Constancy of Regression Relationships Over Time." *Journal of the Royal Statistical Society 37:*149–163, 1975.

41. G. Chow, "Tests of Equality Between Two Sets of Coefficients in Two Linear Regressions." *Econometrica 28*(July):591–605, 1960.

Chapter IV

The Transportation Demand for Energy

INTRODUCTION

The transportation sector uses energy to move people and goods by highway and air. In 1978 in the United States the transportation sector accounted for 26 percent of total energy consumption. Given the likelihood that this percentage will increase as the level of economic activity expands (see Table IV.1 for an indication of the trend since 1965), it becomes essential to investigate whether there are factors that will serve to militate against this trend. In particular, will increases in the price of energy impact transportation usage? Is there an identifiable substitution between energy sources used for transportation?

One of the characteristics of the transportation sector in the United States is that the energy type used is closely related to the transportation mode (or vehicle) which, in turn, provides well-defined transportation services. As an example, diesel fuel is consumed by motor carriers who provide a transportation service (surface cargo transport) that is different from other modes of transportation. Given a specific piece of capital equipment used in the transportation process, interfuel substitution is limited (and for the most part nonexistent). Jet airplanes do not run on electrical energy. To the extent interfuel substitution occurs, it will be the result of capital stock substitution (e.g., automobiles powered by diesel fuel instead of motor

93

Table IV.1. Energy Consumption in the Transportation Sector

Year	Transportation Energy Consumption / Total U.S. Energy Consumption	Energy Expenditures Mix in the Transportation Sector			
		Motor Gasoline	Diesel Fuel	Jet Fuel	Electrical Energy
1965	0.2367	0.96	0.01	0.02	0.01
1966	0.2374	0.96	0.01	0.02	0.01
1967	0.2381	0.94	0.02	0.03	0.01
1968	0.2390	0.94	0.02	0.03	0.01
1969	0.2398	0.94	0.02	0.03	0.01
1970	0.2406	0.94	0.02	0.03	0.01
1971	0.2441	0.93	0.02	0.04	0.01
1972	0.2468	0.93	0.02	0.04	0.01
1973	0.2482	0.92	0.03	0.04	0.01
1974	0.2482	0.90	0.04	0.05	0.01
1975	0.2571	0.89	0.04	0.06	0.01
1976	0.2559	0.88	0.05	0.06	0.01
1977	0.2585	0.88	0.05	0.06	0.01
1978	0.2639	0.87	0.06	0.06	0.01

Source: Department of Energy, Edison Electric Institute, Bureau of Labor Statistics, Platt's Oilgram

gasoline) or switching modes of travel (e.g., motor gasoline for electrical energy by using an automobile instead of taking a subway on the journey to work).

These institutional and technological rigidities would suggest that interfuel substitution would be fairly limited in the transportation sector. Motor gasoline, diesel fuel used for motor vehicles, aviation (jet) fuel, and electrical energy (used in rail travel and by electric vehicles) are typically associated with capital equipment that is not designed for multifuel use.[1]

Given this, the constrained possibility of interfuel substitution will not necessarily preclude the demand for energy responding to relative energy price variations. Instead, capital and/or labor can be substituted for energy. Thus, capital can be substituted for energy through improved energy efficiency (e.g., by smaller and ligher vehicles), while labor can be substituted for energy through the manual mode (e.g., walking).

The expenditure distribution in the transportation sector for various energy forms (motor gasoline, diesel fuel, jet fuel, and electrical energy) is given in Table IV.1 for the aggregate United States over the period 1965 through 1978.[2] Motor gasoline is predominant. It accounted for 96 percent of transportation energy expenditures in 1965. This fell to 87 percent in 1978. Diesel fuel and jet fuel are distant seconds, although they both made significant inroads into transportation energy expenditures over the past decade. Note that diesel fuel is used primarily by buses and trucks whereas motor gasoline is used by automobiles. There is a potential element of interfuel substitution between motor gasoline and diesel fuel. Some automobiles are diesel fueled, and some trucks consume motor gasoline. Moreover, bus travel is a substitute for automobile travel. This must be examined empirically.

Jet fuel consumption has grown rapidly, reflecting the steady increases in air travel. One would expect this trend to continue in light of recent airline deregulation.[3] The use of electrical energy is relatively minor (but not insignificant). There is a very real potential for interfuel substitution between electrical energy and other energy sources. Trains can be powered by diesel engines as well as electric turbines.

In light of the foregoing considerations, the components of energy demand in the transportation sector are examined. In the subsequent three sections the demand for motor gasoline, diesel fuel, and aviation (jet) fuel are studied. It is realized that numerous transportation modes and types of capital equipment exist. The notion of an energy aggregate is unsuitable. Consequently, the total demand for each energy source is investigated separately. After this determination of the aggregate energy demand, the extent of interfuel substitution over the historical period is modeled. This should give some insight into whether changing relative energy prices are affecting energy demand.

MOTOR GASOLINE DEMAND

Background

Undoubtedly the most intensively investigated area of the demand for energy is the one dealing with motor gasoline. A plethora of studies exist.[4] Typically, the studies use either time series analyses or pooled cross-section time series analyses with price and income as explanatory variables. Short-run price elasticities range between -0.06 and -0.47, whereas long-run elasticities vary between -0.48 and -3.80. The income elasticities are somewhat less variable, ranging between 0.30 and 0.74 in the short run and 0.98 and 1.69 in the long run. (See Taylor[5] for a comment on these results.)

The aforementioned studies present problems that have the effect of biasing the price elasticity downward (in absolute terms). United States data over the majority of the sample periods employed contain relatively small variations in the price of motor gasoline. Prior to the 1970s, the price of motor gasoline had been relatively low and automobiles (on a weight basis) were fairly inexpensive. The network of highways and roads, the distribution (spatially) of the population, and the stock of automobiles correspondingly adjusted to these attributes. Until the precipitous price increase in imported crude oil that began in 1973, the automobile industry in the United States had not been wont to produce the smaller-sized, more fuel-efficient vehicle.

Furthermore, most (though not all) of the demand for motor gasoline studies have relied on single equation specifications. For example, Houthakker and colleagues[6] determined the quantity demanded in the current period directly from the quantity demanded in the previous period and price and income in the current period. This approach is remiss in not reflecting the stock of automobiles and its characteristics (e.g., fuel efficiency) in modeling the demand for motor gasoline. Consequently, the adjustment process is obfuscated.

The Model Formulation

Following Cato et al.[7] Griffin,[8] and Ramsey et al.,[9] the demand for motor gasoline consists of three components. These include the utilization rate of an automobile (looked upon as an average across the entire fleet), U; the fuel efficiency, Fe; and the stock of vehicles, S. These are combined to yield X_t, motor gasoline demand in period t, in the following way:

$$X_t = U_t \cdot \frac{S}{Fe}. \qquad (4.1)$$

The strength of examining the demand for motor gasoline in this fashion is that the short-run and long-run elements can be examined independently. Thus, factors affecting the utilization of the existing stock of automobiles will impact motor gasoline more quickly than factors affecting the average efficiency of the stock of automobiles.

The absence of regional data on all of the relevant explanatory variables preclude a highly disaggregated (by state or region) estimation of the functional relationships. Consequently, a U.S. aggregate model is estimated. No attempt is made to disaggregate the data by size of vehicle.

The stock of cars is hypothesized to be a linear in logarithmic function of per capita disposable income, Y_t, and a generalized price computed (following Cato et al.,) as

$$GP = P_S + \sum_{i=0}^{9} \frac{(P_m/MPG)*VM}{(1 + r)_i}, \qquad (4.2)$$

where GP   denotes the generalized price of cars;

     r   denotes the discount rate (which is assumed, following Baumol,[10] to equal 10 percent);

   P_m denotes the price of motor gasoline;

MPG   denotes the average automobile efficiency for new automobiles;

  VM   denotes the vehicle miles traveled per year (which is set equal to 10,000 miles per year, the U.S. national average[11]); and

  P_S denotes the sticker price of cars.

Finally, the demand for automobiles is expressed as

$$\log S_t = \alpha_0 + \alpha_1 \log Y_t + \alpha_2 \log GP_t, \qquad (4.3)$$

where α_0, α_1, and α_2 are parameters to be estimated; log denotes Napierian logarithms; and the other notation is as previously defined.

This demand function implicitly assumes that consumers correctly discount the lifetime cost of motor gasoline associated with the operation of a vehicle. The total stock variable is constructed assuming exponential scrappage. That is, the automobile stock in the current period is a function of the stock in the previous period and the current period new car sales:

$$S_t = NCS_t + 0.92\, S_{t-1}, \tag{4.4}$$

where NCS denotes new car sales. Note, following Sweeny, the annual scrappage rate is estimated to be 8 percent per year.[12] It is this definition of the stock of automobiles that is used in the estimation of relationship (4.3).

The utilization of the automobile stock or the vehicle miles traveled is a function of, among other things, the cost per mile of travel, CPM; income per capita, Y; weather (measured as cooling degree days), W; and the unemployment rate, RU. This last factor is critical in reflecting the impact employment has on the journey to work, which in turn directly affects the utilization of the existing vehicle stock. The inclusion of weather is important given the consumption of motor gasoline in warm weather. The cost per mile is constructed as a simple function of the real price of motor gasoline divided by the average number of miles per gallon of the existing vehicle stock. Thus, the cost per mile is just a function of the gasoline cost.

These considerations give a utilization specification of the form:

$$\log U_t = \beta_0 + \beta_1 CPM + \beta_2 Y_t + \beta_3 RU_t + \beta_4 W_t, \tag{4.5}$$

where β_0, β_1, β_2, and β_3 are parameters to be estimated and the other notation is as previously defined.

The estimation of fleet fuel efficiency is a straightforward process. Assuming exponential scrappage and usage rate, the average miles per gallon of the automobile stock in a given period is a function of last period's automobile stock, the scrappage rate, the utilization rate, and the quantity and miles per gallon of new cars. The concept of adjusting the stock for relative usage reflects the fact that older cars are driven less. Consequently, if new car sales are relatively small, the automobile stock consists of older cars and, assuming a declining utilization rate, the stock will be utilized less than if it had relatively more new cars.

Data

The demand for motor gasoline is measured as the total consumption of motor gasoline. Data on the stock of motor vehicles variable, consisting of passenger car registrations, were obtained from the Federal Highway Administration. It must be realized that some motor gasoline is consumed by vehicles other than passenger cars (e.g., by trucks). It is not, unfortunately, possible to reflect this in the data. Motor gasoline price data came from Platt's Oil Price Handbook and Oilmanac.[13] Data on vehicle miles traveled and efficiency of new automobiles were obtained from the Federal Highway Administration.

The sticker prices of cars came from Milne et al.[14] Motor gasoline price data were obtained from the U.S. Department of Energy, while the unemployment rate information came from the Bureau of Labor Statistics.

The per capita income variable is that reported by the Bureau of Economic Analysis, U.S. Department of Commerce. Note that it incorporates two separate influences. On the one hand, following traditional neoclassical microeconomic theory, the level of income influences the demand for any good or service. On the other hand, it reflects such things as changes in the degree of urbanization and a trend toward multiple car ownership.

All of the data series cover the period 1964–1978. All pecuniary values are in constant (1972) dollar terms.

Estimation Results

Equations (4.3) and (4.5), specified in the foregoing subsection, were estimated via classical least squares analysis, with serial correlation being corrected for via the iterative technique of Cochrane and Orcutt.[15] The results for Eq. (4.3) are given in Table IV.2, while the results for Eq. (4.5) are reported in Table IV.3.

The estimated values are consistent with a priori expectations. In the case of the stock of automobiles, as per capita income increases so does the stock. A 1 percent rise in per capita income gives rise to a 1.22 percent rise in the stock of automobiles. This result is quite a bit smaller than the unrealistically high elasticity estimate of 5.2 obtained by Cato et al. for the United States. Unfortunately, there are few other studies to which this disparity can be judged. One study that does afford a comparative opportunity is that by Chow.[16] He

Table IV.2. Stock of Automobiles

Coefficient	Estimate[1]
α_0	5.9132
	(1.6040)
α_1	1.2189
	(0.5142)
α_2	−0.7612
	(0.2741)
ρ^2	0.3766
	(0.1021)
$\bar{R}^2$	0.9115
D.W.[3]	2.02

Notes:
[1] Standard errors of estimates in parentheses.
[2] Serial correlation coefficient.
[3] Durbin-Watson Statistic.

Table IV.3. Utilization Rate of Automobiles

Coefficient	Estimate[1]
β_0	11.6370
	(5.0173)
β_1	−0.9743
	(0.3188)
β_2	0.2621
	(0.1193)
β_3	−0.0104
	(0.0053)
β_4	0.0218
	(0.0100)
ρ^2	0.6471
	(0.3002)
$\bar{R}^2$	0.9546
D.W.[3]	2.11

Notes:
[1] Standard errors of estimates in parentheses.
[2] Serial correlation coefficient.
[3] Durbin-Watson statistic.

finds income elasticities between 1.4 and 2.0 over the period 1929–1953, which is more consistent with the results obtained here. It is appropriate to question whether an income elasticity in excess of 2 is realistic for a relatively high-income country like the United States. The stock of automobile is large, and the proportion of automobiles to the total population would be expected to increase less rapidly as the saturation level is approached. The effect of rising income is likely to lead to the purchase of higher-quality (in a subjective sense) automobiles and only secondarily to an expansion in the stock of automobiles.

The estimate of the price elasticity is significant and of the correct sign, suggesting that a 1 percent increase in the generalized price results in a −0.76 percent reduction in the automobile stock. This result is only slightly smaller than the −0.96 estimate of Cato et al.

The utilization equation yields interesting results. Most noticeable is the relatively high degree of responsiveness to motor gasoline price changes. The suggestion is that a 1 percent rise in the price of motor gasoline will result in a −0.97 percent decline in miles traveled per vehicle. This estimate is almost precisely the same as the −0.92 value obtained by Wildhorn et al.[17] Cato and associates, on the other hand, obtain an estimate of −0.36. This seems to be a rather low estimate in light of the study of Wildhorn et al. as well as the studies surveyed by Taylor. In this latter group, a value of −0.80 is the norm.

The income elasticity is positive and of approximately the same magnitude as the estimate obtained by the other studies just cited. The one exception is that of Griffin (see note 8), who actually gets a negative estimate on the income term for the Organization for Economic Cooperation and Development (OECD) countries. He argues that income is serving as a proxy for cars per capita, which should exert a negative influence on gasoline consumption. As income increases, cars per capita rise, which in turn leads to lower consumption. The veracity of this argument is not judged here.

The significance of weather in explaining utilization is insightful. The suggestion is that a 1 percent increase in weather leads to a 0.02 percent rise in vehicle miles traveled. This reflects the fact that automobiles are used more intensively in periods of very clement weather. Be cautioned, however, that the inclusion of a weather variable is not reflecting any correction for longer warm-ups during periods of cold weather nor for the operation of air conditioners in warmer periods. This would be reflected in the efficiency parameter.

Finally, the unemployment rate proves to be small but quite significant. In excess of 50 percent of all motor gasoline is consumed on the journey to work.[18] Any reduction in the number of those taking that journey serves to reduce the number of miles traveled and correspondingly reduces the demand for motor gasoline.

What can one glean from the estimation results? The responsiveness of motor gasoline demand to change in the price of motor gasoline is quite significant. This response shows up on two fronts: First, it affects the utilization of automobiles (in the form of vehicle miles traveled). Second, it impacts the stock of automobiles, implicitly changing the characteristics of this stock (toward more fuel efficiency, etc.)

DIESEL FUEL DEMAND

Because of the amorphous composition of the group of consumers of diesel fuel, the determination of demand for diesel fuel is less refined. Lack of adequate data on the characteristics of the consumers of diesel fuel precludes a structure analogous to that used for determining the demand for motor gasoline.

The methodology adopted to model aggregate energy demand is the traditional formulation based on price and economic activity.[19] The appropriateness of these factors is embedded in economic theory. The focus of this investigation is on long-run relationships. (Note that because of this, no short-run adjustment parameter is introduced.) As a result the approach used is that of Houthakker and Taylor, which suggests that diesel fuel demand, D_f, is a linear-in-logarithms function of the level of economic activity (measured by the index of industrial production in real terms), IP. Economic activity is a principal determinant of freight movements. Also the price of diesel fuel relative to the price of all goods and services, P_d, is introduced. In preliminary analyses, to make the results conformable to those in the previous section, weather and the unemployment rate were introduced. Neither proved to be statistically significant. The exact functional specification is thus:

$$\log D_{ft} = \delta_0 + \delta_1 \log IP_t + \sum_{j=0}^{n} \delta_{2j} \log P_{d(t-j)}, \qquad (4.6)$$

where δ_0, δ_1, and δ_{2j} are parameters to be estimated, and the other terms are as previously defined.

A priori one would expect the coefficient on the economic activity variable to be positive, suggesting that increases in freight and passenger movements (which vary coincidentally with industrial production) increase the demand for diesel fuel. In the case of diesel fuel prices, it is a well-understood phenomenon that changes in the price will alter the utilization of the existing stock of trucks and buses in the current period. Additionally, as the price of energy increases relative to the price of capital (i.e., trucks and buses) there will be a replacement of existing (and hence implicitly less energy-efficient) trucks and buses by relatively more energy-efficient rolling stock. Since the replacement process is spread over a number of years, price changes in the current period would be expected to influence the demand for diesel fuel several years hence.

The data requirements to estimate relationship (4.6) are easily satisfied. Information on diesel fuel demand is available from the U.S. Department of Energy, while the price data are available from the Bureau of Labor Statistics, U.S. Department of Labor. The industrial production measure is that compiled by the Federal Reserve Board. To make the estimation horizon consistent with that for motor gasoline demand, the period 1964–1978 is used in the estimation.

The results of the estimation are given in Table IV.4. Various lengths of lag were tried on the price variable using the polynomial distributed lag technique of Almon.[20] A third-order lag using a quadratic polynomial provided the best (in the statistical sense) fit. This is not meant to imply without reservation that the effects of a change in the price of diesel fuel are exhausted after three years—only that the identifiable, measurable effect dissipates. Correction for serial correlation was required.

The importance of the level of economic activity in explaining the demand for diesel fuel is quite transparent. Diesel fuel

Table IV.4. Diesel Fuel Demand

Coefficient	Estimate[1]
δ_0	-0.6171
	(0.2547)
δ_1	0.9955
	(0.4203)
δ_{20}	-0.1536
	(0.0774)
δ_{21}	-0.2190
	(0.1061)
δ_{22}	-0.1839
	(0.0684)
δ_{23}	-0.0942
	(0.0453)
ρ^2	0.4388
	(0.1291)
$\bar{R}^2$	0.9362
D.W.[3]	2.05

Notes:
[1] Standard errors of estimates in parentheses.
[2] Serial correlation coefficient.
[3] Durbin-Watson statistic.

is a normal good, and increased demand is closely linked to rising industrial production. The elasticity is effectively 1, suggesting that as the level of economic activity doubles the quantity of diesel fuel demanded doubles. This is almost equal to the 0.97 value Griffin reports for his 18-century OECD sample.

The diesel fuel price profile is quite significant. The effect of a price change in the current period is to reduce (increase) consumption in the current period by 0.15 for each 1 percent increase (decrease). The impact reaches its peak in the second period, when for each 1 percent change in price in the current period the quantity demanded falls in the next period by 0.22 percent. The aggregate effect of a change in price by 1 percent is to alter the quantity demanded in the opposite direction by 0.65 percent. (Note that the lag structure results because of the degree of the polynomial fit through the coefficients.) This value is consistent with the estimate obtained by the Federal Energy Administration.[21]

THE DEMAND FOR AVIATION FUEL

The aviation fuel component of total transportation fuel expenditures is growing rapidly; in 1978 it was approximately equal in size to diesel fuel demand. Beginning in the early part of the 1960s, jet fuel demand began to be the dominant component of aviation gasoline as jet aircraft replaced propeller driven aircraft. Consequently, the demand for aviation fuel is used synonymously with the demand for jet fuel.

To date, a comprehensive model of the demand for jet fuel reflecting the institutional structure of the industry does not exist.[22] Data problems seem prohibitive. As a result, a simple specification analogous to that used to explain the demand for diesel fuel is adopted. In particular, the aviation demand for fuel, D_a, is hypothesized to be a function of the level of economic activity (measured as per capita income), Y, and the price of jet fuel, P_j. Moreover, due to the significant increase in aviation fuel demand not reflected in these two factors, an exponential trend variable, t, is introduced. This yields the exact functional form

$$\log D_{at} = \Theta_0 + \Theta_1 \log Y_t + \Theta_2 \log P_{jt} + \Theta_3 t. \qquad (4.7)$$

We can anticipate that an increase in the level of economic activity will have a positive effect on fuel demand. Moreover, to the extent air line travel is a superior good, the coefficient estimate might very well exceed 1. In studying the demand for air travel in the United States between 1947 and 1965, Phillips found an income elasticity of 1.45.[23] The impact of jet fuel price changes on the quantity demand, if the aforementioned study by the Federal Energy Administration (FEA) is any indication,[24] will be small and negative. Higher fuel prices raise the cost of air travel, thereby reducing revenue passenger miles and hence the demand for aviation fuel.

The quantity data used in the estimation process were obtained from the U.S. Department of Energy, while the jet fuel price data came from the Bureau of Labor Statistics, U.S. Department of Labor. The disposable income information was supplied by the Bureau of Economic Analysis, U.S. Department of Commerce. Both price and income are in constant dollars over the period 1964–1978.

Table IV.5 reports the estimation results with the appropriate correction for serial correlation made. The importance of the level of economic activity as a determinant of aviation fuel consumption is clearly demonstrated. The price elasticity likewise is significant and, as expected, relatively small. The price of jet fuel is serving as a proxy for other factors. Finally, the significant time trend is just reflecting the movement toward increased air travel.

THE TRANSPORTATION DEMAND FOR ELECTRICAL ENERGY

The last major energy source used to be considered here is electrical energy. This is accounted for primarily by rail travel. Because it is relatively small, the causal factors influencing it have not been subjected to any consistent investigation. Con-

Table IV.5. Aviation Fuel Demand

Coefficient	Estimate[1]
θ_0	3.9182 (0.9462)
θ_1	1.3619 (0.5221)
θ_2	−0.1374 (0.0556)
θ_3	0.0104 (0.0049)
ρ^2	0.1363 (0.0625)
$\bar{R}^2$	0.8466
D.W.[3]	2.10

Notes:
[1] Standard errors of estimates in parentheses.
[2] Serial correlation coefficient.
[3] Durbin-Watson statistic.

sequently, an ad hoc specification is adopted whereby the demand for electrical energy in the transportation sector, D_{eet}, is a linear-in-logarithms function of the price of electrical energy to that secotor, P_{eet}, as well as the level of economic activity, Y. This gives an exact specification of the form

$$\log D_{eet} = \phi_0 + \phi_1 \log Y_t + \phi_2 \log P_{eet} \qquad (4.8)$$

where ϕ_0, ϕ_1, and ϕ_2 are parameters to be estimated and the other factors are as previously defined. Note that, from Table IV.1, due to the absence of any identifiable trend, no factor representing a movement toward more intensive rail travel has been included. Analogous to the previous results, we would anticipate a positive coefficient on the economic activity (disposable income) variable.

The effect of an increase in the price of electrical energy on the quantity demanded should be negative. Higher energy prices raise the cost of rail travel, reducing the number of revenue passenger miles and hence the demand for electrical energy by the transportation sector.

The quantity and price data used to estimate relationship (4.8) were obtained from the Edison Electric Institute, while the disposable income data came from the Bureau of Economic Analysis, U.S. Department of Commerce. Both price and income are in constant dollars over the period 1964 to 1978.

The estimation results are given in Table IV.6. (Note the required correction for serial correlation.) There are no surprises. The level of economic activity directly affects the quantity of electrical energy consumed by the sector, while price and the quantity demanded are inversely related. The fairly sizeable coefficient on the disposable income factor would suggest that electric rail travel is a superior good.

INTERFUEL SUBSTITUTION

Background

The approach used to describe interfuel substitution in the transportation sector is to consider the issue as one of minimizing the costs of satisfying a given level of aggregate energy demand—subject, of course, to the institutional constraints.

Table IV.6. Electrical Energy
Transportation Demand

Coefficient	Estimate[1]
Φ_0	-0.4604
	(0.2037)
Φ_1	0.8435
	(0.4113)
Φ_2	-0.3021
	(0.1063)
ρ^2	0.2190
	(0.0948)
$\bar{R}^2$	0.8172
D.W.[3]	1.94

Notes:
[1] Standard errors of estimates in parentheses.
[2] Serial correlation coefficient.
[3] Durbin-Watson statistic.

Given this, an energy cost function, P_E, is hypothesized that depends on motor gasoline, diesel fuel, jet fuel, and electrical energy:

$$P_E = \Omega(P_m, P_d, P_j, P_{ee}), \qquad (4.9)$$

where P_m, P_d, P_j, and P_{ee} denote the prices of motor gasoline, diesel fuel, jet fuel, and electrical energy, respectively. It is desirable to specify a general functional form which has a minimal number of a priori restrictions. The translog price-possibility frontier allows a large degree of generality since it places no restrictions on the Allen partial elasticities of substitution and can be viewed as a second-order approximation to any arbitrary twice-differentiable price-possibility frontier.[25]

The translog price-possibility frontier for the energy price aggregate is expressed as follows:

$$\log P_E = \alpha_o + \sum_i \alpha_i \log P_i$$
$$+ \tfrac{1}{2} \sum_i \sum_k \gamma_{ik} \log P_i \log P_k \qquad (i, k = m, d, j, ee), \quad (4.10)$$

where the α's and γ's are unknown parameters; m, d, j, and ee refer to motor gasoline, diesel fuel, jet fuel, and electrical energy, respectively; P_E is the price of energy; and the P_i's are the prices of the energy sources. In order to correspond to a well-behaved cost function, a price-possibility frontier must be homogeneous of degree 1 in prices; that is, for a fixed-level aggregate energy demand, total energy expenditures must increase proportionately when all fuel prices increase proportionately. This implies the following relationships among the parameters:

$$\sum_i \alpha_i = 1 \tag{4.11}$$

and

$$\sum_i \gamma_{ik} = 0 \qquad (i, k = m, d, j, ee). \tag{4.12}$$

A convenient feature of the price-possibility frontier approach is that the derived demand functions for the fuels can be easily computed by partially differentiating relationship (4.10) with respect to the energy price; that is,

$$\frac{\partial P_E}{\partial P_i} = X_i. \tag{4.13}$$

This result, known as Shephard's lemma,[26] is conveniently expressed in logarithmic form for the translog price-possibility frontier as follows:

$$\frac{\partial \log P_E}{\partial \log P_i} = \frac{P_i X_i}{\sum_k P_k X_k} = S_i \qquad (i, k = m, d, j, ee), \tag{4.14}$$

where S_i indicates the cost share of the ith energy source. The translog price-possibility frontier yields the cost-share equations as follows:

$$S_m = \alpha_m + \gamma_{mm} \log P_m + \gamma_{md} \log P_d$$
$$+ \gamma_{mj} \log P_j + \gamma_{mee} \log P_{ee} \tag{4.15a}$$

$$S_d = \alpha_d + \gamma_{dm} \log P_m + \gamma_{dd} \log P_d$$
$$+ \gamma_{dj} \log P_j + \gamma_{dee} \log P_{ee} \tag{4.15b}$$

$$S_j = \alpha_j + \gamma_{jm} \log P_m + \gamma_{jd} \log P_d$$
$$+ \gamma_{jj} \log P_j + \gamma_{jee} \log P_{ee} \tag{4.15c}$$

$$S_{ee} = \alpha_{ee} + \gamma_{eem} \log P_m + \gamma_{eed} \log P_d$$
$$+ \gamma_{eej} \log P_j + \gamma_{eeee} \log P_{ee}. \tag{4.15d}$$

Note that the cost shares sum to 1.

The application of Shephard's lemma implies that energy prices are exogenously determined from the transportation sector. Given this, actual energy prices can be used in the estimation process without introducing the concern over simultaneous equation bias. The markets for motor gasoline, diesel fuel, and jet fuel are nationwide and worldwide. The market for electrical energy is regulated. Consequently, transportation sector consumption should have little appreciable influence on the delivered prices of the various types of energy.

Uzawa[27] has shown that Allen[28] partial elasticities of substitution between energy sources are given by the formula

$$\sigma_{ik} = \frac{\Omega_E \cdot \Omega_E^{ik}}{\Omega_E^i} \cdot \Omega_E^i \cdot \Omega_E^k, \tag{4.16}$$

where the superscripts on Ω_E indicate the partial differentiation of the cost function (4.10) with respect to the energy prices. For the translog price-possibility frontier, one has

$$\sigma_{ii} = \frac{\gamma_{ii} + S_i^2 - S_i}{S_i^2} \tag{4.17a}$$

and

$$\sigma_{ik} = \frac{\gamma_{ik} + S_i S_k}{S_i S_k} \quad (i \neq k) \quad \text{for } i, k = m, d, j, ee. \tag{4.17b}$$

Further, Allen (note 28) has shown that the elasticities of substitution are related to the price elasticities of demand for energy, η_{ik}, as

$$\eta_{ik} = S_k \sigma_{ik}. \tag{4.18}$$

This formulation assumes that $\Sigma_k \eta_{ik} = 0$ because of linear homogeneity in energy prices.

The partial elasticities of substitution are invariant with regard to the ordering of the energy input factors. Therefore, $\sigma_{ik} = \sigma_{ki}$, although in general $\eta_{ik} \neq \eta_{ki}$.

Before proceeding, it is instructive to reflect upon just what it is that is the objective of the estimation. The purpose here is to derive estimates of long-run interfuel substitution possibilities and estimates of the price elasticities of demand. The translog formulation is a means to that end, not an end in itself.

Estimation Procedure

It is feasible to estimate the parameters of the price-possibility frontier using ordinary least squares analysis. This technique is certainly attractive from the point of view of simplicity. It neglects, however, the additional information contained in the share equations, which are also easily estimable. Furthermore, even for a modest number of factor prices the translog price-possibility frontier has a large number of regressors which do not vary greatly across regions. Hence multicollinearity may be a problem, resulting in imprecise parameter estimates.

An alternative estimation procedure, and the approach used here, is to jointly estimate the cost-share equations as a multivariate regression system. This procedure is satisfactory since the cost-share equations include all of the parameters of the price-possibility frontier except the constant and no information is lost by not including the price-possibility frontier in the estimation procedure.

Additive disturbances are specified for each of the share equations. Since the cost-share equations are derived by differentiation, they do not contain the disturbance term from the cost function. It is assumed that the disturbances have a joint normal distribution. Following Zellner,[29] nonzero correlations across time are allowed. Unfortunately, his proposed estimation procedure is not operational for the model described here. The estimated disturbance covariance matrix required to implement Zellner's procedure is singular because the disturbances on the share equations must sum to zero. The Zellner procedure can be made operational by deleting one of the share equations from the system. However, the estimates so obtained will not be invariant in regard to which equation is deleted.

Barten[30] has shown that maximum likelihood estimates of a system of share equations with one equation deleted are invariant in regard to which equation is dropped. Kmenta and Gilbert[31] have shown that iteration of the Zellner estimation procedure until convergence results in maximum likelihood estimates. Iterating the Zellner procedure is a computationally efficient method for obtaining maximum likelihood estimates and is the procedure which is employed here.

Data

The share equations are estimated using time series data covering the period 1964 through 1978. The data were obtained from the sources previously enumerated for the energy-source-specific demand models.

Empirical Results

The maximum likelihood estimates are invariant with regard to which equation is omitted. Consequently, Eqs. (4.15a) through (4.15c) were estimated and the coefficient estimates of (4.15d) derived from these. Linear homogeneity in fuel prices constraints [i.e., relationships (4.11) and (4.12)] have been imposed. Additional regularity conditions which the price-possibility frontier must satisfy in order to correspond to a well-behaved cost structure are monotonicity and convexity in energy prices. Sufficient conditions for these are positive fitted cost shares and negative definiteness of the bordered Hessian matrix of the price-possibility frontier. These conditions are met at most observations for the model estimated; hence it is concluded that the estimated price possibility frontier represents a well-behaved cost structure.

Serial correlation, as with most time series models, proved to be a problem and so had to be corrected for in each estimated share equations.

One additional issue presents itself: Are the parameters on the share equations symmetric? That is, does $\gamma_{ik} = \gamma_{ki}$? To test for symmetry, which implies that an increase in the price of energy source k will affect the expenditure share on energy type i to the same extent as a rise in the price of energy type i affects the expenditure on energy source k, a Quandt test is employed. The test consists of the following steps:

Denote the determinants of the unrestricted and restricted estimates of the disturbance covariance matrix by $|\hat{\Sigma}_u|$ and $|\hat{\Sigma}_r|$ when Eqs. (4.15a) through (4.15c) are estimated. The likelihood ratio becomes

$$\beta = \left(\frac{|\hat{\Sigma}_u|}{|\hat{\Sigma}_r|}\right)^{-T/2}, \tag{4.19}$$

where T is the number of observations. The hypothesis is tested using the fact that $-2 \log \beta$ has a chi-square distribution with degrees of freedom equal to the number of independent restrictions being imposed.[32] The test was performed with the null hypothesis being that symmetry holds. The determinant of the unconstrained covariance matrix was 178.333 while the determinant of the constrained covariance matrix was 177.942, indicating that the null hypothesis cannot be rejected at the 95 percent level.

Moreover, a preliminary examination of the results suggested that the serial correlation coefficient was equal across share equations. This constraint was imposed and the Quandt test employed. Assuming that symmetry is valid, the serial correlation constrained logarithm determinant was 177.647, suggesting that the effect of serial correlation is the same across share equations.

Following from the results of these two tests, the reported empirical estimates impose the symmetry constraint and equality of serial correlation constraint across share equations. The results are given in Table IV.7.

All of the own-price coefficient estimates are significantly different than zero at the 95 percent level. The cross-price coefficients, on the other hand, are in general not. In view of the overall inability to substitute transportation modes, this is not surprising. Note that the nature of the translog function does not allow the precise testing of zero price elasticities.

Estimates of the average price elasticities of demand are given in Table IV.8. (Since the estimates of the elasticities of substitution provide little added insight, they are not reported.) Own-price elasticities should be negative, and cross-price elas-

Table IV.7. Parameter Estimates for the Translog Energy Expenditures Shares Model

Parameter	Estimate[1]
α_m	0.3760 (0.0882)
α_d	0.2864 (0.1039)
α_j	0.3239 (0.1463)
α_{ee}	0.0137 (0.0017)
γ_{mm}	−0.0136 (0.0065)
γ_{dd}	−0.0306 (0.0144)
γ_{jj}	−0.0236 (0.0101)
γ_{eeee}	−0.0142 (0.0073)
γ_{md}	0.0102 (0.0045)
γ_{mj}	0.0006 (0.0369)
γ_{mee}	0.0028 (0.0562)
γ_{dj}	0.0160 (0.0099)
γ_{dee}	0.0044 (0.0021)
γ_{jee}	0.0070 (0.0163)
ρ^2	0.9396 (0.0274)

Notes:
[1] Standard errors of estimates in parentheses.
[2] Serial correlation coefficient.

Table IV.8. Elasticities of Demand
for the Transportation Sector

Elasticity	Estimate
η_{mm}	-0.3510^*
η_{dd}	-0.4563^*
η_{jj}	-0.1174^*
η_{eeee}	-0.2494
η_{md}	0.1261^*
η_{mj}	-0.0366
η_{mee}	-0.0014
η_{dm}	0.1634^*
η_{dj}	0.0263
η_{dee}	0.0536^*
η_{jm}	0.0163
η_{jd}	-0.0154
η_{jee}	0.0547
η_{eem}	-0.0632
η_{eed}	0.0479^*
η_{eej}	0.0261

Note:
* Significant at the 90 percent level or better.

ticities should be positive. In the case of the significant estimates, this is precisely the pattern that evolves.

There is considerable variation with regard to the energy price elasticities. The differences follow from the properties of Eqs. (4.15a) through (4.15d) and (4.18) and the negative coefficients for γ_{mm}, γ_{dd}, γ_{jj}, and γ_{eeee}.

The transportation sector is truly responding to price changes. Note, however, that the magnitude of the response is not the same in both directions. This is a reflection of methodology used in computing the price elasticities as well as the facility with which one can switch to alternative energy sources.

What is the mechanism through which the observed interfuel substitution can be made? First, the absolute decline in the consumption of a specific energy type is accomplished by improving the energy efficiency of the existing stock of equipment. Thus, by purchasing smaller, more efficient automobiles and discarding the relatively more inefficient, an absolute reduction in energy consumption is realized.

Next, changing energy prices alters the marginal costs of operating various types of transportation equipment, which provides an incentive to search for improvements in operating norms. Thus, reducing the average speed at which an automobile is driven (e.g., from 65 miles per hour to 55 miles per hour) or altering the angle of an aircraft on takeoff will result in a net reduction in the quantity of energy demanded.

Finally, as the prices of the various types of energy change relative to one another, and as this change is explicitly reflected in the transportation charges, there is an impetus to shift modes. Thus, as the price of motor gasoline increases relative to the price of diesel fuel, the journey to work via private automobile becomes relatively more expensive than via diesel-fueled buses (i.e., public transportation).

In attempting to make comparisons between the interfuel elasticity estimates obtained here and those calculated elsewhere, once again a dearth of studies exists. One that provides estimates that are conformable is the Annual Report to Congress (1980).[33] In this study, respective estimates of -0.29, -0.66, and -0.42 for motor gasoline, diesel fuel, and jet fuel own-price elasticities are reported. The only cross-price elasticity given is a value of -0.37 between motor gasoline and diesel fuel. The methodology employed is not precisely delineated, so it is difficult to offer a conjecture as to why, in particular, the jet fuel own-price elasticity and the motor gasoline–diesel fuel cross-price elasticity are so divergent.

As previously observed, a nice theoretical property of the translog formulation is that the sum of own- and cross-price elasticities among energy types is zero. It is instructive to consider the magnitude of the cross-price elasticities in order to determine the main channels of interfuel substitution. Table 4.8 reports these elasticities. The effects of higher oil prices and consequently higher diesel fuel prices will offer a stimulus to electrical energy consumption. This will be in the form of increased rail travel, as consumers shift away from trucks and buses toward trains.

TESTING FOR MODEL STABILITY

Major attention has focused on the demand for energy in the transportation sector. Of major concern in the context of drawing meaningful inferences over the historical period as well as over any forecast horizon is whether the observed relationships (i.e., price elasticities) are stable. (Stability is defined in the statistical sense of the estimated coefficients of the explanatory variables remaining constant over time.) Policy inferences are made on the basis of past behavior. If the functional relationship has been subject to change, then necessarily the inferences will be, at least in part, unsatisfactory.

The purpose of this section is to examine the question of the existence of a stable demand for energy types utilizing a statistical test developed by Brown et al.[34] The approach is adopted in deference to others available (e.g., the Chow test[35]) because it does not require prior knowledge of the shifts. Rather it tests for the presence of such occurrences over the sample period.

To give an appreciation of the aforementioned test, it is now briefly discussed. A way of investigating this time variation of a regression coefficient is to fit the regression as a short segment of n successive observations and to move this segment along the series. A significance test for constancy based on this approach is derived from the results of regressions based on nonoverlapping time segments. The method relies on a test statistic which equals the difference between the sum of squared residuals of the entire sample less the cumulative sum of squared residuals over the nonoverlapping segments divided by the cumulative sum of squared residuals of the nonoverlapping segments. The null hypothesis that the regression relationship is constant over time implies that the value of the test statistic is distributed as F. Specifically, consider the time segments for a moving regression of length $n - (1, n)$, $[(n + 1), (2n)]$, $\ldots$, $[(p - 1) n + 1, T]$, where p is the integral part of T/n and the variance ratio considered (i.e., the homogeneity statistic) is

$$\omega = \frac{T - kp}{kp - k} \frac{S(1, T) - \Delta}{\Delta}, \qquad (4.20)$$

where k is the number of regressors; Δ = {S(1, n) + [S(n + 1), 2n] + $\cdots$ + [(pn − n + 1), T]}; and S(r, s) is the residual sum of squares from the regression calculated from observations t = r to s inclusive. This is equivalent to the usual "between groups over within groups" ratio of mean squares and under H_o is distributed as F(kp − k, T − kp).

Relying on the previous discussion, the objective is to explicitly test for the stability of the demand for energy in the transportation sector over the period 1965–1978. Dividing the data into two equal length intervals (i.e., n = 7, p = 2) allows for the computation of the test statistic for each of the share equations. As noted, one of the equations must be deleted, and as before the electrical energy equation was selected. The tabulated value of ω, the test statistic, using Eq. (4.20) for the three share equations, is given in Table IV.9. The results are fairly conclusive. None of the share equations are unstable over the period 1965–1978.

The implications of these results for estimating the demand for energy in the transportation sector are clear. Events since 1965 have left virtually unchanged the demand for motor gasoline, diesel fuel, jet fuel, and (implicitly) electrical energy. That is, for the energy types used in the transportation sector, the relative importance of the price of motor gasoline, diesel fuel, jet fuel, and electrical energy in influencing the share of total expenditures (and hence demand) has remained constant.

One must be careful, however, to avoid inferring that the quantity demanded of energy has not changed. The estimation results clearly show that the price of the various energy types (in particular motor gasoline versus diesel fuel and aviation fuel versus electrical energy) influences expenditure shares. The magnitude of this response in the aggregate remained

Table IV.9. Computed Value of the Stability Test Statistic ω

Share Equation	Computed Value of ω	Tabulated Critical Value [1]
1. Motor Gasoline	3.61	6.26
2. Diesel Fuel	3.84	6.26
3. Jet Fuel	4.23	6.26

Note:
[1] That is, $F_{0.05}$ (5,4).

unaltered over the sample period. Another way of expressing this is to say that the share elasticities for the energy source did not vary.

CONCLUSIONS

There is considerable potential for energy conservation in the transportation sector in the United States. Even though the substitution among energy types is limited essentially to motor gasoline and diesel fuel, there is also the potential to substitute between modes using alternative energy sources.[36]

Our efforts in the foregoing analysis have been directed at examining the effect of energy prices on the quantity of energy demanded. For motor gasoline, the suggestion is that vehicle miles traveled as well as the stock of automobiles respond to changing motor gasoline prices. For diesel fuel consumption, aviation fuel consumption, and electrical energy, it is the case that the quantity of energy demanded does respond to energy prices as well as the level of economic activity. The magnitude of the price responsiveness is typically small, given that energy costs are but a minor portion of truck, bus, air, and rail transport costs.

NOTES AND REFERENCES

1. Note that the use of electrical energy by vehicles accounted for less than 0.1 percent of total generation in 1978. See, e.g., H.R. Glixon, *The Current Status of the Electric Vehicle*, U.S. Department of Energy, Washington, 1981.

2. Note that while it might be desirable to report regional data, conformable times series do not exist.

3. E.E. Bailey, "Reform from Within: Civil Aeronautics Board Policy 1977–1978," in *Problems in Public Utility Economics and Regulation*, M.A. Crew (ed.). Lexington, Mass.: D.C. Heath and Company, 1978.

4. For a survey see D.L. Green and A.B. Rose, *The ORNL Highway Gasoline Demand Model*. Oak Ridge, Tenn.: Oak Ridge National Laboratory, 1980.

5. L.D. Taylor, *The Demand for Energy*. Tucson: University of Arizona, 1976.

6. H.S. Houthakker, P.K. Verglager, and D.P. Sheehan, "Dynamic Demand Analysis for Gasoline and Residential Electric." *American Journal of Agricultural Economics 56*:321–329, 1974.

7. D. Cato, M. Rodekohr, and J. Sweeney, "The Capital Stock Adjustment Process and the Demand for Gasoline: A Market Share Approach," in

Econometric Dimensions of Energy Demand and Supply, A.B. Askin and J. Kraft (eds.). Lexington, Mass.: D.C. Heath and Company, 1976.

8. J.M. Griffin, *Energy Conservation in the OECD: 1980 to 2000.* Cambridge, Mass.: Ballinger Publishing Company, 1979.

9. J.B. Ramsey, R. Rasche and B. Allen, "An Analysis of the Private and Commercial Demand for Gasoline." *The Review of Economics and Statistics* 57:233–240, 1975.

10. W.J. Baumol, "On the Social Rate of Discount." *The American Economic Review 58:*788–802, 1968.

11. J.L. Staley, *Transportation Energy Use.* New York: Garland Publishing Garland Publishing, Inc., 1979.

12. J. Sweeney, *Passenger Car Use of Gasoline.* Washington, D.C.: Federal Energy Administration, 1975.

13. *Platt's Oil Price Handbook and Oilmanac.* New York: McGraw-Hill, Inc. Annual.

14. J.A. Milne, C. Cantwell and H. Eissler, *Automobile Characteristics Historical Data Base.* Radnor, Pa.: Chilton and Company, (ND)

15. D. Cochrane and G.H. Orcutt, "Applications of Least Squares Regressions to Relationships Containing Autocorrelated Error Terms." *Journal of the American Statistical Association 44:*31–62.

16. G. Chow, "Statistical Demand Functions for Automobiles and Their Use in Forecasting," in *The Demand for Durable Goods,* A. Harberger (ed.). Chicago: The University of Chicago Press, 1960.

17. S. Wildhorn, B.K. Burright, J.H. Ennis and T.F. Kirkwood, *How to Save Gasoline: Public Policy Alternatives for the Automobile.* Santa Monica, Calif.: The Rand Corporation, 1974.

18. D.J. Kulash, "Energy Efficiency: Which Modes, Which Programs?", in *Transportation and Energy,* American Society of Civil Engineers (ed.). New York: American Society of Civil Engineers, 1978.

19. H.S. Houthakker and L.D. Taylor, *Consumer Demand in the United States.* Cambridge, Mass.: Harvard University Press, 1970.

20. S. Almon, "The Distributed Lag Between Capital Appropriations and Expenditures." *Econometrica 33:*178–196, 1965.

21. Federal Energy Administration, *National Energy Outlook.* Washington, D.C.: U.S. Government Printing Office, 1976.

22. J. O'Brien, *Modeling the Aviation Demand for Energy.* Washington, D.C.: U.S. Department of Energy, 1981.

23. A. Phillips, *Technology and Market Structure.* Lexington, Mass.: D.C. Heath and Company, 1971.

24. The FEA obtains a price elasticity of −0.25.

25. L.R. Christensen, D.W. Jorgensen and L.J. Lau, "Transcendental Logarithmic Production Frontiers." *The Review of Economics and Statistics* 55(February):28–45, 1973.

26. R.W. Shephard, *Cost and Production Functions.* Princeton, N.J.: Princeton University Press, 1963.

27. H. Uzawa, "Production Functions with Constant Elasticities of Substitution." *The Review of Economics and Statistics 44*(October):291–299, 1962.

28. R.G.D. Allen, *Mathematical Analysis for Economists.* London: Macmillan and Company, 1938.

29. A. Zellner, "An Efficient Method of Estimating Seemingly Unrelated Regression and Tests for Aggregation Bias." *Journal of the American Statistical Association* 57(June):348–368, 1962.

30. A.P. Barten, "Maximum Likelihood Estimation of a Complete System of Demand Equations." *European Economic Review* 1(Fall): 7–73, 1969.

31. J. Kmenta and R.F. Gilbert, "Small Sample Properties of Alternative Estimators of Seemingly Unrelated Regressions." *Journal of the American Statistical Association* 63(December):1180–1200, 1968.

32. S. Goldfeld and R.E. Quandt, *Nonlinear Methods in Econometrics.* Amsterdam: North-Holland Publishing Company, 1972.

33. U.S. Department of Energy, *The Annual Report to Congress.* Washington, D.C.: U.S. Government Printing Office, 1980.

34. R.L. Brown, J. Durbin and J.M. Evans, "Techniques for Testing the Constancy of Regression Relationships Over Time." *Journal of the Royal Statistical Society* 37:149–163, 1975.

35. G. Chow, "Tests of Equality Between Two Sets of Coefficients in Two Linear Regressions." *Econometrica* 28(July):591–605, 1960.

36. D.V. Harper, *Transportation in America.* Englewood Cliffs, N.J.: Prentice-Hall, Inc., 1978.

Chapter V

The Demand for Energy
By Electric Utilities

INTRODUCTION

The generation of electrical energy constitutes a major consumer of primary energy (coal, oil, and natural gas). Moreover, electrical energy is a major energy source to residential and commercial, industrial, and transportation consumers. For the aggregate United States, electrical energy accounts for about 7.3 percent of total energy Btu's (British thermal units) and about 27.4 percent of total energy expenditures. There is considerable regional variability, however, in these averages. Table V.1 gives the relative importance of electrical energy as a percentage of total energy consumed by region for 1978. As a consumer of fuels, the electric utility sector is an even larger consumer of primary energy because of the thermal efficiency in converting conventional fossil fuels into electrical energy. Only one-third of the fossil fuel is converted to usable (by end-use consumers) Btu's of electrical energy.[1]

As indicated in the third column of Table V.1, the generation of electrical energy is a large consumer of coal in most regions (the New England, West South Central, and Pacific regions excepted). That is, regionally, the generation of electrical energy accounts for up to 83 percent of the total quantity of coal consumed by all sectors. Additionally, electrical energy generation consumes a significant percentage of natural gas and oil (distillate fuel oil, crude oil, and residual fuel oil). There

123

Table V.1. Electrical Energy End Use Consumption and Fuel Consumption for 1978 (in Percent)

| Region | Electrical Energy Consumption | Electrical Energy Expenditure | Coal Consumption | Oil Consumption | Natural Gas Consumption |
	Total Energy Consumption	*Total Energy Expenditures*	*Total Fuel Consumption*	*Total Fuel Consumption*	*Total Fuel Consumption*
1. New England	6.64	25.57	4.43	75.48	1.24
2. Middle Atlantic	6.85	28.37	39.68	41.00	4.29
3. East North Central	6.89	27.05	82.61	5.11	5.89
4. West North Central	6.12	26.11	52.20	2.52	31.97
5. South Atlantic	9.01	28.88	54.69	28.93	9.17
6. East South Central	10.31	28.64	75.61	1.57	8.18
7. West South Central	5.49	26.65	1.74	2.19	94.37
8. Mountain	6.84	25.28	39.77	2.64	28.04
9. Pacific	8.91	26.91	0.25	13.33	27.18

Source: Bureau of Mines, Edison Electric Institute.

is considerable variability between regions due to a myriad of reasons including fuel availability, hydroelectric potential, the relative price of fuels, environmental constraints, etc.[2] The Pacific region, for example, produces 56.9 percent of its electrical energy with hydroelectric power. Looking at the aggregate United States, electric utilities in 1978 consumed 77.5 percent of all coal, 17.91 percent of all natural gas, and 7.80 percent of all petroleum as primary energy.

Upon reflecting on the data, the concern here is with identifying the potential for interfuel substitution between fossil fuels. The generation of electrical energy is well suited for such an examination. Generation is based on a capital stock with a long (30- to 50-year) life.[3] In general, the ability to burn alternative fuels is limited. Consequently, the response to changing relative fuel prices is through the utilization of the existing capacity, that is, through changing the merit order of individual plants.[4] Consequently, if the price of oil rises relative to the price of coal and natural gas, the plants utilizing the latter fuels will be used more intensively. Over a longer term, it is possible to retrofit conventional boilers to burn the alternative, relatively cheaper fuel. (As an aside, note that it is less costly to convert from coal to oil or natural gas than the other way around, i.e., from natural gas to oil to coal. This has to do with technical considerations as to boiler design. For some generating units, as the relative price of the boiler fuel rises to a given level it is optimal to retire the boiler.[5]

De facto, energy substitution in the generation of electrical energy is a long-term phenomenon. If it is the case, as typically assumed in econometrics,[6] that interregional variation explains long-term responses and intraregional variations capture short-term responses, the empirical results should reflect these responses for electrical energy generation.

Given this objective, the following section will outline theoretical constructs of the model to be used and the assumptions inherent in the determination of energy and fuel response. In the succeeding section, aggregate energy inputs are determined in the electrical energy generation sector. Attention will focus on the elasticity of substitution between energy and the other factor inputs (capital and labor). Next, interfuel substitution possibilities are examined. Finally, the implications are presented.

THEORETICAL BACKGROUND

It is assumed that the electric utility sector has a twice-differentiable production function relating the generation of electrical energy, Q, to technological change, t, and the factor inputs capital, K, labor, L, and three energy types, coal, C, natural gas, G, and oil (including residual fuel oil, distillate fuel oil, and crude oil[7]), O:

$$Q = \phi(K, L, C, G, O, t). \tag{5.1}$$

Note that Q is only reflecting fossil fuel generation excluding hydroelectric, nuclear, and geothermal generation. The latter are treated as exogenous. The focus, for now, is only on fossil fuel generation.

Corresponding to the production function is a well-balanced cost function

$$\Omega = \Omega(P_K, P_L, P_C, P_G, P_O, t, Q), \tag{5.2}$$

where P_K, P_L, P_C, P_G, and P_O are, respectively, the input prices of capital, labor, coal, natural gas, and oil.[8]

In the analysis to follow, it is assumed that coal, natural gas, and oil constitute a separable and homogeneous energy aggregate, E, allowing relationship (5.2) to be restated as

$$\Omega = \Omega(P_K, P_L, \Omega_E(P_C, P_G, P_O), t, Q) \tag{5.3}$$

or

$$\Omega = \Omega(P_K, P_L, P_E, t, Q) \tag{5.4}$$

with

$$P_E = \Omega_E(P_C, P_G, P_O), \tag{5.5}$$

where P_E denotes the price of the energy aggregate.

Thus, Ω is stated as two separate submodels—one in which capital, labor, and aggregate energy inputs are determined, and a second submodel in which specific fuel inputs are determined. Note that relationship (5.5) directly influences the aggregate energy input choice through P_E in Eq. (5.4).[9]

The sufficient conditions for this specification are important.[10] Separability requires that the ratio of the cost shares of any two fossil fuels be independent of the prices outside the aggregate energy input such as capital and labor. De facto, the ratio of the shares depends just on fuel prices. This is not an unrealistic assumption since capital cost for a coal-fired plant is approximately the same as the cost of a natural gas-fired plant.[11] Linear homogeneity in input prices in relationships (5.4) and (5.5) in turn implies that the cost shares of fuels are independent of total expenditure on the energy inputs. Jorgensen and Berndt (see note 9) use this assumption to permit the estimation of relationships (5.4) and (5.5) and consequently conserve degrees of freedom. In the present instance this assumption is made to allow the estimation of Ω_E independent of the estimation of Ω because of data limitations. Based on the results of Atkinson and Halvorsen[12] this does not seem to be an unwarranted assumption.

AGGREGATE ENERGY INPUTS

This section concerns itself with the aggregate demand for energy inputs in the production process, i.e., the generation of electrical energy. To represent the cost function in relationship (5.4), the constant elasticity of substitution (CES) specification of Arrow et al. is selected.[13] This formulation presumes that the same elasticity of substitution, σ' holds among capital, labor, and energy. The CES cost function is given as

$$C = \left(\frac{Q}{\lambda e^{\gamma t}}\right)^{1/v} [\delta_0^\sigma P_K^{1-\sigma} + \delta_1^\sigma P_L^{1-\sigma} + (1 - \delta_0 - \delta_1)^\sigma P_E^{1-\sigma}]^{1/(1-\sigma)}, \quad (5.6)$$

where γ is the technological efficiency coefficient; λ is the rate of Hicks neutral technical change; δ_0, δ_1, and $(1 - \delta_0 - \delta_1)$ are distributional coefficients on the factors of production; and the other terms are as previously defined. Observe that the parameter v measures returns to scale so that v equaling 1 implies constant returns to scale.

If data were available for regional capital and labor costs, relationship (5.6) could be directly estimated. Unfortunately, time series data for the nine regions do not exist. It is possible, however, to determine energy input requirements given data on generation, Q, and the price of electrical energy through the derived demand equation for energy. Corresponding to the CES cost function is the CES production function of the form

$$Q = \gamma e^{\lambda t} [\delta_0 K^{-\zeta} + \delta_1 L^{-\zeta} + (1 - \delta_0 - \delta_1) E^{-\zeta}]^{-v/\zeta}, \quad (5.7)$$

where $\zeta = (1 = \sigma)/\sigma$.

The marginal product of energy is

$$\frac{\partial Q}{\partial E} = v(1 - \delta_0 - \delta_1) (\gamma e^{\lambda t})^{-\zeta/v} \frac{Q(1 + \zeta)/v}{E^{1+\zeta}}. \quad (5.8)$$

Using the standard microeconomic theoretic assumptions,[14] the value of the marginal product will equal the price of energy; that is,

$$P_E = \frac{\partial Q}{\partial E} \cdot P_{EE}, \quad (5.9)$$

where P_E isthe price of electrical energy.

Substituting relationship (5.8) into relationship (5.9) and rearranging terms one has

$$E = [v(1 - \delta_0 - \delta_1)]^{1/(1+\zeta)} (\gamma e^{\lambda t})^{-\zeta/v(1+\zeta)} Q^{(v+\zeta)/v(1+\zeta)} \left[\frac{P_{EE}}{P_E}\right]^{1/(1+\zeta)} \quad (5.10)$$

Taking logarithms and simplifying (substituting for δ), the demand for aggregate energy becomes

$$\log E = C^* - \frac{\lambda(1 - \sigma)}{v} t + \frac{v\sigma + 1 - \sigma}{v} \log Q + \sigma \log \frac{P_{EE}}{P_E}, \quad (5.11)$$

where C^* is a constant and log denotes Napierian logarithms.

The data enabling us to estimate relationship (5.11) come from various issues of the *Statistical Yearbook* of the Edison Electric Institute[15] and cover the years 1956 through 1977. Here E, total energy inputs, is measured in Btu's. Because Btu's are equivalent in thermal efficiency in steam generation, no thermal efficiency adjustment was necessary. Generation, Q, is simply total fossil fuel fired generation converted from kilowatt-hours to Btu's. The price of electrical energy, P_{EE}, is difficult to measure since average price measures (to specific sectors or overall) include distribution costs as well as generation costs. Since the price of electrical energy to the industrial sector has the smallest distributional component,[16] it most closely approximates the pure generation cost. The price of energy, P_E, is simply a weighted average of fuel costs per Btu of electrical energy generation.

The results of the estimation are given in Table V.2. Since the relationship is nonlinear in the parameters, a maximum likelihood estimation technique was used. Serial correlation, based on the computed Durbin–Watson statistic, did not seem to be a problem and consequently was not corrected for. The data were pooled across regions utilizing both interregional and intraregional variation.

All of the estimates are highly significant. A value for σ of -0.24 is quite significantly different from zero, suggesting that the technology is not characterized by a Leontief fixed-coefficient production function. That is, labor, capital, and energy are substitutable for one another. This is consistent with results of the study by Griffin,[17] that found substitution occurs between capital and energy in the design of more efficient equipment. It also occurs in the use of newer, more energy-efficient equipment versus the use of older, less energy-efficient equipment. This arises primarily due to the necessity of satisfying peak seasonal electrical energy requirements. Gas turbines, which minimize capital costs at the expense of a very inefficient

Table V.2. Aggregate Energy Input for Electrical Energy Generation

Coefficient	Estimate[1]
Constant	68.9885
	(15.5153)
ν	0.9814
	(0.0464)
σ	-0.2392
	(0.0313)
λ	0.0226
	(0.0033)
$\bar{R}^2$	0.9998
D.W. Statistic[2]	2.0529

Notes:
[1] Standard errors of estimates in parentheses.
[2] Durbin-Watson Statistic.

fuel use are preferred for meeting peak loads since they are in operation only a few months during the year. Under such circumstances, the capital cost per hour of operation is high relative to fuel costs. For baseload generation these relative costs are not as great, but we would still expect capital–energy substitution to occur.

An equally significant finding is that the returns to scale coefficient v is not significantly different than unity, which implies the presence of constant returns to scale. This might seem surprising at first given the fairly large literature showing economies of scale over a wide range of output.[18]

One explanation for this finding follows recent evidence of Scherer[19] and the earlier work of Nerlove.[20] Both studies suggest the widely found tendency of economies of scale to exist over smaller plants. Beyond the initial range of economies of scale, however, the long-run average cost function for generation is virtually horizontal. Plants with a capacity of greater than 600 megawatts are likely to have taken full advantage of any economies of scale. If the major portion of new generation capacity is of optimal size, then for the electric utility sector in each region constant returns to scale would be observed.[21]

One difficulty with this explanation is that, if demand is insufficient to warrent plants greater than 600 megawatts in size, the smaller regions (in physical size) might have higher electrical energy output ratios. Thus, when pooled across regions, increasing returns would be indicated.

Even in such a situation, the returns-to-scale parameter would unlikely be much lower than 1. Barzel (using a nonhomothetic production function) shows that scale effects are significantly stronger for labor and capital inputs than for fuel inputs.[22] Using a sample of varying plant sizes, he found that the elasticities of substitution for capital and labor with regard to plant size were 0.82 and 0.63, respectively. For energy inputs, this elasticity was 0.90. Given these results and the tendency for the elasticity of substitution to approach 1 for larger plants, the estimate obtained here represents at most a small upward bias. The results of Atkinson and Halvorsen (as previously noted) and Christensen and Greene[23] also support this conclusion.

FUEL SHARE DETERMINATION

Background

Given a determination of the demand for total regional fossil fuel, the next step is a determination of the fuel mix between coal, oil, and natural gas. It is desirble to specify a general functional form which has a minimal number of a priori restrictions. The translog price-possibility frontier allows a large degree of generality since it places no restrictions on the Allen partial elasticities of substitution and can be viewed as a second-order approximation to any arbitrary twice-differentiable price possibility frontier.[24]

The translog price-possibility frontier for the energy price aggregate is expressed as follows:

$$\log P_E = \alpha_0 + \sum_i \alpha_i \log P_i + \tfrac{1}{2} \sum_i \sum_j \gamma_{ij} \log P_i \log P_j$$

$$(i, j = C, O, G), \tag{5.12}$$

where the α's and γ's are unknown parameters; C, O, G refer to coal, oil, and gas, respectively, P_E is the price of energy; and the P_i's are the prices of the fuel inputs. In order to correspond to a well-behaved production function, a price-possibility frontier must be homogeneous of degree 1 in prices; that is, for a fixed level of output, total energy expenditures must increase proportionately when all fuel prices increase proportionately. This implies the following relationship among the parameters:

$$\sum_i \alpha_i = 1 \tag{5.13}$$

$$\sum_i \gamma_{ij} = 0 \qquad (i, j = C, O, G). \tag{5.14}$$

A convenient feature of the price-possibility frontier approach is that the derived demand functions for the fuel inputs can be easily computed by partially differentiating relationship (5.12) with respect to the fuel prices; that is,

$$\frac{\partial P_E}{\partial P_i} = X_i. \tag{5.15}$$

This result, known as Shephard's lemma,[25] is conveniently expressed in logarithmic form for the translog price possibility frontier as follows:

$$\frac{\partial \log P_E}{\partial \log P_i} = \frac{P_i X_i}{\Sigma P_j X_j} = S_i \qquad (i, j = C, O, G), \qquad (5.16)$$

where S_i indicates the cost share of the ith fuel input. The translog price-possibility frontier yields the cost-share equations as follows:

$$S_C = \alpha_C + \gamma_{CC} \log P_C + \gamma_{CC} \log P_G + \gamma_{CO} \log P_O, \qquad (5.17a)$$

$$S_O = \alpha_O + \gamma_{OC} \log P_C + \gamma_{OG} \log P_G + \gamma_{OO} \log P_O, \qquad (5.17b)$$

$$S_G = \alpha_G + \gamma_{GC} \log P_C + \gamma_{GG} \log P_G + \gamma_{GO} \log P_O. \qquad (5.17c)$$

Note that the cost shares sum to unity.

The application of Shephard's lemma implies that fuel prices are exogenously determined from the electric utility sector. Given this, actual fuel prices can be used in the estimation process without introducing the concern over simultaneous equation bias. The markets for coal, oil, and natural gas are nationwide and worldwide. Consequently, the electric utilities in a specific region have little discernible impact on the delivered prices of the fuels.

Uzawa[26] has shown that Allen partial elasticities of substitution between fuel inputs[27] are given by the formula

$$\sigma_{ij} = \frac{\Omega_E \cdot \Omega_E^{ij}}{\Omega_E^i \cdot \Omega_E^i \cdot \Omega_E^j}, \qquad (5.18)$$

where the superscripts on Ω_E indicate the partial differentiation of the energy submodel (5.5) with respect to the fuel prices. For the translog price-possibility frontier, we hve

$$\sigma_{ii} = \frac{\gamma_{ii} + S_i^2 - S_i}{S_i^2} \qquad (5.19a)$$

$$\sigma_{ij} = \frac{\gamma_{ij} + S_i S_j}{S_i S_j} \qquad (i \neq j) \qquad \text{for } i, j = C, O, G. \qquad (5.19b)$$

Further, Allen[27] has shown that the elasticities of substitution are related to the price elasticities of demand for the fuel inputs, η_{ij}, as

$$\eta_{ij} = S_j \sigma_{ij}. \qquad (5.20)$$

This formulation assumes that $\Sigma_j \, \eta_{ij} = 0$ because of linear homogeneity in fuel prices.

The partial elasticities of substitution are invariant with regard to the ordering of the fuel input factors. Therefore $\sigma_{ij} = \sigma_{ji}$, although in general $\eta_{ij} \neq \eta_{ji}$.

Before proceeding, it is instructive to reflect upon just what it is the objective of the present estimation. The purpose here is to derive estimates of long-run regional interfuel substitution possibilities and estimates of the price elasticities of demand. The translog formulation is a means to that end, not an end in itself.

Estimation Procedure

It is feasible to estimate the parameters of the price-possibility frontier using ordinary least squares analysis. This technique is certainly attractive from the point of view of simplicity. It neglects, however, the additional information contained in the share equations, which are also easily estimable. Furthermore, even for a modest number of factor prices the translog price-possibility frontier has a large number of regressors which do not vary greatly across regions. Hence multicollinearity may be a problem, resulting in imprecise parameter estimates.

An alternative estimation procedure, and the approach used here, is to jointly estimate the cost-share equations as a multivariate regression system. This procedure is satisfactory since the cost-share equations include all the parameters of the price-possibility frontier except the constant and no information is lost by not including the price-possibility frontier in the estimation procedure.

Additive disturbances are specified for each of the share equations. Since the cost-share equations are derived by differentiation, they do not contain the disturbance term from the cost function. It is assumed that the disturbances have a joint normal distribution. Following Zellner,[28] nonzero correlations across regions are allowed but zero correlations across time are imposed. However, his proposed estimation procedure is not operational for the model. The estimated disturbance covariance matrix required to implement Zellner's procedure is singular because the disturbances on the share equations must sum to zero for each region. The Zellner procedure can be made operational by deleting one of the share equations from the system. However, the estimates so obtained will not be invariant to which equation is deleted.

Barten[29] has shown that maximum likelihood estimates of a system of share equations with one equation deleted are invariant in regard to which equation is dropped. Kmenta and Gilbert[30] have shown that iteration of the Zellner estimation procedure until convergence results in maximum likelihood estimates. Iterating the Zellner procedure is a computationally efficient method for obtaining maximum likelihood estimates and is the procedure which is employed here.

Data

The share equations are estimated with pooled annual data compiled by Census region[31] for the period 1961–1978. Both price and quantity of fuel data consumed by electric utilities over this period were obtained from the National Coal Association.[32]

Note that regional coefficients were not included in the estimating equations because the estimation procedure captures interregional variation through the variance–covariance matrix.

Finally, natural gas curtailments became a significant consideration in 1973.[33] Preliminary analysis, however, did not indicate that the cost shares were appreciably affected.

Empirical Results

The maximum likelihood estimates are invariant with regard to which equation is omitted. Consequently, Eqs. (5.17a) and (5.17c) were estimated and the coefficient estimates of (5.17b) derived from these. Linear homogeneity in fuel prices constraints, i.e., Eqs. (5.13) and (5.14), have been imposed. Additional regularity conditions which the price-possibility frontier must satisfy in order to correspond to well-behaved production structures are monotonicity and convexity in fuel prices. Sufficient conditions for these are positive fitted costs shares and negative definiteness of the bordered Hessian matrix of the price-possibility frontier. These conditions are met

at most observations for the model estimated; hence it is concluded that the estimated price-possibility frontier represents
a well-behaved production structure.

Serial correlation, as with most time series models, proved
to be a problem and hence had to be corrected for in each
estimated share equation.

One additional issue presents itself: Are the parameters on
the share equations symmetric? That is, does $\gamma_{ij} = \gamma_{ji}$? To test
for symmetry, which implies that an increase in the price of
fuel j will affect the expenditure share on fuel i to the same
extent as a rise in the price of fuel i affects the expenditure
on fuel j, a Quandt test is employed. The test consists of the
following steps:

Denote the determinants of the unrestricted and restricted
estimates of the disturbance covariance matrix by $|\hat{\Sigma}_u|$ and $|\hat{\Sigma}_r|$
when Eqs. (5.17a) and (5.17c) are estimated. The likelihood
ratio becomes

$$\beta = \left(\frac{|\hat{\Sigma}_u|}{|\hat{\Sigma}_r|}\right)^{-T/2}, \tag{5.21}$$

where T is the number of observations. The hypothesis is
tested using the fact that $-2 \log \beta$ has a chi-square distribution
with degrees of freedom equal to the number of independent
restrictions being imposed.[34] The test was performed with the
null hypothesis being that symmetry holds. The determinant
of the unconstrained covariance matrix was 627.022 while the
determinant of the constrained covariance matrix was 626.849,
indicating the null hypothesis cannot be rejected at the 95
percent level.

Moreover, a preliminary examination of the results suggested that the serial correlation coefficient was equal across
share equations. This constraint was imposed and the Quandt
test employed. Assuming that symmetry is valid, the serial
correlation constrained determinant was 626.809, suggesting
that the effect of serial correlation is the same across share
equations.

As a result of these two tests, the reported empirical estimates
impose the symmetry constraint and equality of serial correlation constraint across share equations. The results are given

in Table V.3. All of the estimates are significantly different than zero at the 95 percent level, leading to the conclusion that price elasticities and elasticities of substitution are not zero.

Estimates of the average elasticities of substitution for the period 1961–1978 based upon cost shares are presented in Table V.4 and average regional price elasticities of demand over the period are presented in Table V.5. Own-price elasticities should be negative, and cross-price elasticities should be positive. This is precisely the pattern that evolves. Note that the computed values are fairly representative of the last few years, given the relatively stable nature of the cost shares.

Table V.3. Parameter Estimates for the Translog Fuel Model

Parameter	Estimate[1]
α_C	0.0841 (0.0405)
α_O	0.6588 (0.1769)
α_G	0.2571 (0.1073)
γ_{CC}	−0.1203 (0.0549)
γ_{OO}	−0.0713 (0.0348)
γ_{GG}	−0.1027 (0.0392)
γ_{CO}	0.0431 (0.0197)
γ_{CG}	0.0745 (0.0360)
γ_{OG}	0.0282 (0.0116)
ρ^2	0.9762 (0.0127)

Notes:
[1] Standard errors of the estimate in parentheses.
[2] Serial correlation coefficient.

Table V.4. Regional Elasticities of Substitution for the Period 1961–1978

Region	σ_{CC}	σ_{OO}	σ_{GG}	σ_{CG}	σ_{CO}	σ_{OG}
1. New England	−19.16[1]	−0.09	*	*	0.55	*
2. Middle Atlantic	−1.56	−0.31	*	*	0.94	*
3. East North Central	−0.21	−0.70	*	*	0.19	*
4. West North Central	−0.25	*	−0.06	0.10	*	*
5. South Atlantic	−1.92	−0.22	−1.20	1.12	0.09	0.48
6. East South Central	−0.22	−0.68	*	*	0.29	*
7. West South Central	*	−0.15	−0.35	*	*	0.04
8. Mountain	−0.64	−0.31	−1.32	1.00	0.84	1.75
9. Pacific	*	−0.72	−9.32	*	*	2.61
Total United States	−1.28	−0.73	−1.32	1.28	1.14	1.68

Notes:
* Estimates of the elasticities are omitted since the particular fuel accounted for less than 5 percent of total cost share over the period 1953–1978. In such a situation it is a maintained hypothesis that the estimates are of little significance.
[1] Coal plants in New England weere rapidly phased out in the latter part of the 1960's due to non-economic reasons resulting in large computed own-price and cross-price elasticities.

137

Table V.5. Regional Price Elasticities of Demand for the Period 1961–1978

Region	η_{CC}	η_{OO}	η_{GG}	η_{CO}	η_{CG}	η_{OC}	η_{OG}	η_{GC}	η_{GO}
1. New England	-2.56^1	-0.38	*	2.02	*	1.52	*	*	*
2. Middle Atlantic	-1.58	-0.99	*	0.75	*	0.58	*	*	*
3. East North Central	-0.27	-2.11	*	0.72	*	2.14	*	*	*
4. West North Central	-0.89	*	-0.69	*	0.79	*	*	1.16	*
5. South Atlantic	-0.93	-0.80	*	0.42	*	0.89	*	*	*
6. East South Central	-0.28	-1.10	*	0.42	*	1.94	*	*	*
7. West South Central	*	-0.51	-0.11	*	*	*	0.81	*	0.31
8. Mountain	-1.09	-1.35	-1.44	0.51	0.60	0.42	0.75	0.76	0.96
9. Pacific	*	-0.45	-1.35	*	*	*	0.33	*	1.14
Total United States	-0.97	-0.83	-1.40	1.26	0.53	1.27	0.64	1.25	1.39

Note:
*, [1] See notes on Table 5.2.

One observes a wide variation in regional price elasticities of demand in Table V.4. The differences are attributable entirely to the fuel share composition within that region. For example, the West South Central region, with the highest cost share of natural gas in 1978 (75 percent), has the most inelastic demand for natural gas (-0.11), whereas the West North Central region, with a cost share of 11 percent, has a price elasticity of -0.69. The results follow from the properties of Eqs. (5.19a), (5.19b) and (5.20), (5.11b), and the negative estimated coefficients for γ_{CC}, γ_{OO}, and γ_{GG}.

Electric utilities in the various regions are truly responding to price changes, though the response is not equal in both directions. This arises primarily because of the technology involved in changing existing multifuel plants from one fuel to another. Take as an example the Middle Atlantic region, where it is much easier to shift a multifuel coal–oil plant (which accounted for 26 percent of conventional fossil generation in 1978) from coal to oil as opposed to reversing the process by shifting from oil to coal. The cross-price elasticity in the former case is 0.75, versus 0.58 in the latter case. In the South Atlantic region, on the other hand, the cross-price elasticities are of roughly equal size, with the shift between fuels being more clearly dictated by relative price changes than by the facility with which the change can be made.

The Mountain region deserves special recognition. In 1978, 77 percent of installed fossil capacity was multifuel: coal and oil plants accounted for 7 percent of this; coal and gas plants accounted for 33.5 percent of this; and combined coal, oil, and gas plants accounted for 11 percent. Coal, oil, and gas are all in competition with each other as a fuel for electrical energy generation, and every indication from the results point to the fact that utilities are responsive to relative price changes when making their fuel choice.

Just how does this interfuel substitution occur in the short run? First, individual generating units may be able to utilize more than one type of fuel. Secondly, a plant generally contains more than one generating unit, and different units may utilize different fuels. Consequently, interfuel substitution can occur through changes in the merit order of individual units. Units are brought on line in rank order according to their marginal cost of generation (see Turvey[35]). Changes in fuel prices alter the relative marginal cost of units using different fuels and hence affect the proportion of output produced with each type of fuel. Additionally, even if substitution were not possible at the plant level it might occur at the firm level due to changes in the merit order of plants using different fuels. Similarly, the existence of integrated power pools makes possible further interfuel substitution through reallocations of generation requirements between utilities using different fuels.

It has been argued that fuel adjustment clauses encourage the use of fuels covered by such clauses and the construction of plants burning those fuels and that this discourages development of alternative energy sources.[36] Fuel adjustment clauses move a major component of generating expenses—fuel costs— from rate case proceedings where the utility is subject to cross-examination by commimssion staffs and interested citizens. It is seen from these results that this argument is not totally supportable as utilities did move to cheaper fuels as relative fuel prices changed in the period 1961–1978.

The estimates in Table V.5 provide a basis for the calculation of average elasticities for all regions. Long-run own-price elasticities for the entire United States were -0.97, -0.83, and -1.40 for coal, oil, and gas, respectively. These are comparable to price elasticity estimates found by Griffin[37] for 20 countries. They indicate much larger elasticity estimates than found in other studies. If our results presented here are true, the policy significance is of great importance.

Time series analyses in particular have tended to find oil demand to be very inelastic. For example, Hudson and Jorgenson,[38] when applying the translog approach to the energy subsector of the electric utility industry, report price elasticities for 1969 of -0.45, -0.67, and -0.59 for coal, oil, and gas, respectively. The comparison of the results derived here and those of Hudson and Jorgenson is particularly interesting since it tends to confirm the suspicion that the earlier pure time series approach captured only a portion of the long-run price response in industries involving long periods for capital turnover as in electric utilities.

As previously observed, a nice theoretical property of the translog formulation is that the sum of own- and cross-price elasticities among fuels is zero. It is instructive to consider the magnitude of the cross-price elasticities in order to determine the main channels of interfuel substitution. Table V.5 reports these elasticities. The effect of higher oil prices, say, will create an approximately equal stimulus to both coal and natural gas consumption. In view of the minor share of gas in most regions, together with the much larger share of coal, the primary alternative source to oil will be coal. There is considerable regional variation in this observation, but in the aggregate it is correct.

The study by Hudson and Jorgenson for the electric utility sector provides a basis for comparison of cross-price elasticities as well. Based on 1969 estimates, these investigators find the elasticity of the demand for gas with respect to the price of oil to be 0.20 and the elasticity of demand for coal with respect to the price of oil to be 0.43. The elasticity of the demand for coal with respect to the price of gas is -0.20, indicating complementarity. While the standard errors of their estimates are not given, it seems unrealistic to assume the latter result is statistically significant. In all three cases, the results obtained here indicate compartively greater interfuel substitution effects.

TESTING FOR MODEL STABILITY

Major attention has focused on the demand for fuel inputs in the generation of electrical energy. Of major concern in the context of drawing meaningful inferences over the historical period as well as over any forecast horizon is whether the observed relationships (i.e., price elasticities) are stable. (Stability is defined in the statistical sense of the estimated coefficients of the explanatory variables remaining constant over time.) Policy inferences are made on the basis of past behavior. If the functional relationship has been subject to change, then necessarily the inferences will be, at least in part, unsatisfactory.

The purpose of this section is to examine the question of the existence of a stable demand for fuel inputs utilizing a statistical test developed by Brown et al.[40] The approach is adopted in deference to others available (e.g., the Chow test[41]) because it does not require prior knowledge of the shifts rather tests for the presence of such occurrences over the sample period.

To give an appreciation of the test, it is now briefly discussed. A way of investigating the time-variation of a regression coefficient is to fit the regression on a short segment of n successive observations and to move this segment along the series. A significance test for constancy based on this approach is derived from the results of regressions based on nonoverlapping time segments. The method relies on a test statistic which equals the difference between the sum of squared residuals of the entire sample less the cumulative sum of squared residuals of the nonoverlapping segments divided by the cumulative sum of squared residuals of the nonoverlapping segments. The null hypothesis that the regression relationship is constant over time implies that the value of the test statistic is distributed as F. Specifically, consider the time segments for a moving regression of length n − (1, n), [(n + 1), (2n)], $\cdots$, [(p − 1) n + 1, T], where p is the integral part of T/n and the variance ratio considered (i.e., the homogeneity statistic) is

$$\omega = \frac{T - k_p}{kp - k} \frac{S(1, T) - \Delta}{\Delta}, \qquad (5.21)$$

where k is the number of regressors; $\Delta = \{S(1, n) + [S(n + 1), 2n] + \cdots + [(pn − n + 1), T]\}$; and S(r, s) is the residual sum of squares from the regression calculated from observatons from t = r to s inclusive. This is equivalent to the usual "between groups over within groups" ratio of mean squares and under H_o is distributed as F (kp − k, T − kp).

Relying on the previous discussion, the objective is to explicitly test for the stability of the demand for fossil fuels in the electric utility sector over the period 1961–1978. Dividing the data into nine equal length intervals (i.e., p = 18 and n = 9) allows for the computation of the test statistic for each of the share equations. What is done is equivalent to pooling across all nine regions for a given year and then examining the stability across years. As noted, one of the equations must be deleted and as before the oil equation was selected.

The computed value of ω via Eq. (5.21), the test statistic, for the two share equations is given in Table V.6. The results are quite conclusive. Neither the equation for the demand for coal nor the equation for the demand for natural gas by electric utilities is unstable for over the period 1961–1978.

Table V.6. Computed Value of the Stability Test Statistic ω

Share Equation	Computed Value of ω	Tabulated Critical Value[1]
1. Coal	0.0874	1.48
2. Natural Gas	0.6072	1.48

Note:
[1] That is, $F_{0.05}$ (90, 68).

The implications of the results are clear for estimating the energy submodel for electric utility fuel demands. Events over the past two decades have left virtually unchanged the demand for coal and natural gas (and implicitly the demand for oil). That is, for the factor inputs, the relative importance of the price of coal, the price of natural gas, and the price of oil in influencing the share of total expenditures (and hence demand) has remained constant.

We must be careful, however, to avoid inferring that the quantity demanded of coal, natural gas, and oil has remained unchanged. The estimation results clearly show that the price of all of the fuels influences each expenditure's share. Thus, an increase in the price of coal does lead to an increase in the quantity of natural gas used in the generation process. The magnitude of this response for each of fuel inputs in the aggregate remained unaltered over the sample period. Another way of expressing this is that the share elasticities for the fuels did not vary.

CONCLUSIONS

The generation of electrical energy is an important consumer of primary energy. It is also critical to the energy substitution question since fuels are more easily substituted in this sector than in others.

The approach used to determine the various fossil fuel inputs is a two-step procedure in which, first, aggregate energy demand is determined, followed by determination of corresponding fuel shares. The separation of the fuel determination from aggregate energy input demand suggests that energy is separable and forms a homogeneous aggregate.

In calculating aggregate energy inputs, a constant elasticity of substitution technology is assumed with variable returns to scale and Hicks' neutral technical change. Upon pooling the data across regions, the suggestion emerged showing a nonzero substitution elasticity between energy and other inputs. The technology obeyed constant returns to scale.

The translog fuel share formulation yielded evidence to support the contention that between-region variation shows long-run responses while within-region variation is emulating short-run responses. The former pattern is plausible and has provided considerably more elastic estimation of price elasticities than have U.S. aggregate time series observations.

Finally, the question of the stability of the demand for fuel inputs is addressed. The results are conclusive, suggesting that the demand for coal, natural gas, and oil has remained virtually constant over the past two decades.

NOTES AND REFERENCES

1. Department of Energy, *Annual Report to Congress, 1979,* Volume II. Washington, D.C.: U.S. Government Printing Office, 1980.
2. See N.D. Uri, "The Impact of Environmental Regulations on the Pricing and Allocation of Electrical Energy." *Journal of Environmental Management* 5:215–227, 1977.
3. N.D. Uri, *Towards an Efficient Allocation of Electrical Energy.* Lexington, Mass.: D.C. Heath and Company, 1975.
4. R. Turvey, "Peak Load Pricing." *Journal of Political Economy* 76:101–113, 1968.
5. N.D. Uri, *New Dimensions in Public Utility Pricing.* Greenwich, Conn.: JAI Press Inc., 1981.
6. J. Kmenta, *Elements of Econometrics.* New York: The Macmillan Company, 1971.
7. Distillate fuel oil and crude oil are of minor importance, accounting for less than 5 percent of the total oil consumed. See N.D. Uri, "Forecasting Electric Utility Fossil Fuel Consumption." *Energy* 5:1155–1162, 1980.
8. W.E. Diewart, *Application of Duality.* Department of Manpower and Immigration, Canada, 1973.
9. D.W. Jorgenson and E.R. Berndt, "Production Structure," in *Energy Resources and Economic Growth,* edited by D.W. Jorgenson and H.S. Houthakker. Lexington, Mass.: D.C. Heath and Company, 1973.
10. E.R. Berndt and L.R. Christensen, "The Internal Structure of Functional Relationships–Separability, Substitution and Aggregation. *The Review of Economic Studies* 40:403–410, 1973.
11. N.D. Uri, *Towards an Efficient Allocation of Electrical Energy.* Lexington, Mass.: D.C. Heath and Company, 1975.

12. S.E. Atkinson and R. Halvorsen, "Interfuel Substitution in Conventional Steam-Electric Power Generation." *Journal of Political Economy* (forthcoming).

13. K.J. Arrow, H.B. Chenery, B.S. Minhas, and R.M. Solow, "Capital-Labor Substitution and Economic Efficiency." *The Review of Economics and Statistics 33:*225–250, 1961.

14. J. Henderson and R.E. Quandt, *Microeconomic Theory*, 2nd ed. New York: McGraw-Hill Book Company, 1971.

15. Edison Electric Institute, *Statistical Yearbook*. New York: Edison Electric Institute, Annual.

16. Foster Associates, *Energy Prices*. Cambridge, Mass.: Ballinger Publishing Company, 1973.

17. J.M. Griffin, "The Effects of Higher Prices on Electricity Consumption." *The Bell Journal of Economics and Management Science 5:*515–539, 1974.

18. See M. Gallatin, *Economies of Scale and Technological Change in Thermal Power Generation*. Amsterdam: North-Holland Publishing Company, 1968.

19. C.R. Scherer, *Estimating Electric Power System Marginal Cost*. Amsterdam: North-Holland Publishing Company, 1979.

20. M. Nerlove, "Returns to Scale in Electricity Supply," in *Identification and Estimation of Cobb-Douglas Production Function*. Chicago: Rand McNally and Company, 1968.

21. W. Seitz, "Productive Efficiency in the Steam Electric Generating Industry." *Journal of Political Economy 77*(July):878–886, 1971.

22. Y. Barzel, "The Production Function and Technical Change in the Steam Power Industry." *Journal of Political Economy 62*(April):133–150, 1964.

23. L. Christensen and W. Greene, "Economies of Scale in U.S. Electric Power Generation." *Journal of Political Economy 84*(July):655–676, 1976.

24. L.R. Christensen, D.W. Jorgenson and L.J. Lau, "Transcental Logarithmic Production Frontiers." *The Review of Economics and Statistics 55*(February):28–45, 1973.

25. R.W. Shephard, *Cost and Production Functions*. Princeton, N.J.: Princeton University Press, 1963.

26. H. Uzawa, "Production Functions with Constant Elasticities of Substitution." *The Review of Economies and Statistics 44*(October):291–299, 1962.

27. R.G.D. Allen, *Mathematical Analysis for Economists*. London: Macmillan and Company, 1938.

28. A. Zellner, "An Efficient Method of Estimating Seemingly Unrelated Regression and Tests for Aggregation Bias." *Journal of the American Statistical Association 57*(June):348–368, 1962.

29. A.P. Barten, "Maximum Likelihood Estimation of a Complete System of Demand Equations." *European Economic Review 1*(Fall):7–73, 1969.

30. J. Kmenta and R.F. Gilbert, "Small Sample Properties of Alternative Estimators of Seemingly Unrelated Regressions." *Journal of the American Statistical Association 63*(December):1180–1200, 1968.

31. The regional classification is as follows: (1) New England (Maine, New Hampshire, Vermont, Massachusetts, Rhode Island, Connecticut); (2) Middle Atlantic (New York, New Jersey, Pennsylvania); (3) East North Central (Ohio, Indiana, Illinois, Michigan, Wisconsin); (4) West North Central (Minnesota, Iowa, Missouri, North Dakota, South Dakota, Nebraska, Kansas); (5) South Atlantic (Delaware, Maryland, and the District of Columbia, Virginia, West Virginia, North Carolina, Georgia, Florida); (6) East South Central (Arkansas, Louisiana, Oklahoma, Texas); (8) Mountain (Montana, Idaho, Wyoming, Colorado, New Mexico, Arizona, Utah, Nevada); and (9) Pacific (Washington, Oregon, California).

32. National Coal Association, *Steam Electric Plant Factors*. Washington, D.C.: National Coal Association, Annual.

33. Even though the first natural gas curtailments occurred in 1970, the percentage of natural gas used by electric utilities to fire conventional fossil plants did not measurably decline until 1973 and then only by 3 percent over the historical average.

34. S. Goldfeld and R.F. Quandt, *Nonlinear Method in Econometrics*. Amsterdam: North-Holland Publishing Company, 1972.

35. R. Turvey, *Optimal Pricing and Investment in Electricity Supply*. Cambridge, Mass.: The MIT Press, Inc., 1968.

36. F. Gollop and S. Karlson, *The Impact of the Fuel Adjustment Mechanism on Economic Efficiency*. Madison: The University of Wisconsin, 1979.

37. J.M. Griffin, *Energy Conservation in the OECD: 1980 to 2000*. Cambridge, Mass.: Ballinger Publishing Company, 1979.

38. E. Hudson and D.W. Jorgenson, "U.S. Energy Policy and Economic Growth." *The Bell Journal of Economics and Management Science* 5(Autumn):461–514, 1974.

39. Energy Information Administration, *Annual Report to Congress, 1979*. Washington, D.C.: U.S. Government Printing Office, 1980.

40. R.L. Brown, J. Durbin and J.M. Evans, "Techniques for Testing and Constancy of Regression Relationship Over Time." *Journal of the Royal Statistical Society 37*:149–163, 1975.

41. G. Chow, "Tests of Equality Between Two Sets of Coefficients in Two Linear Regressions." *Econometrica 28*(July):591–605, 1960.

Chapter VI

An Overview of the Energy Demand Analysis System

INTRODUCTION

The foregoing chapters have developed behavioral equations of the demand for energy by four sectors—the residential sector (including residential, commercial, governmental, mining, and agricultural), the industrial sector, the transportation sector, and the electric utility sector. The Energy Demand Analysis System (EDAS) consists of these behavioral equations together with a set of identities.

The subsequent section provides an overview of the structure of the EDAS with emphasis on the level of detail and the important exogenous variables. It must once again be emphasized that the EDAS is designed to be an aggregate forecasting and simulation tool.

STRUCTURE OF THE SYSTEM

Figure VI.1 details the structure of the EDAS. The exogenous variables—including economic activity, weather, and fuel prices—are the EDAS drivers. (Note that the drivers in the current context are variables whose change induces responses in the factors of interest in the EDAS.) These variables have an impact on the energy-consuming sectors. In these sectors aggregate energy requirements are determined by various measures of

Figure VI.1 Energy Demand Analysis System

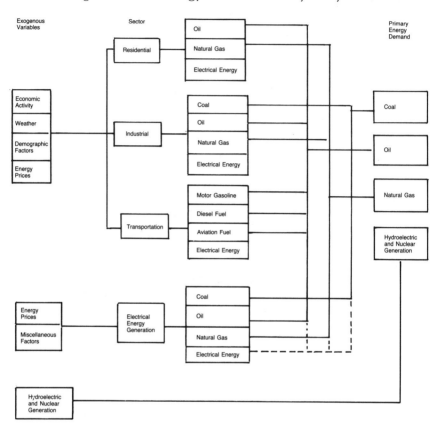

economic activity, the relative price of energy to all other goods and services, weather, and population. Given aggregate energy consumption by each sector, the specific types of energy are determined as a function of relative energy prices, which are exogenous. (This is required since supply-side considerations have been excluded from the previous analysis.)

The production of energy is a significant consumer of energy. One of the components of this—the refining of petroleum products—is included as part of the industrial sector. Losses must be accounted for, however. Electrical energy generation losses, another important component, will be modeled in the next section.

The final energy demand is determined once the energy requirements in the residential, industrial, transportation, and electric utilities sectors are ascertained. It is important to emphasize that final primary energy demand is a reflection of the end use of energy types and not intermediate uses. In Figure VI.1, the final demand for coal, oil, and natural gas is obtained by aggregating energy demand across the individual sectors.

The generation of electrical energy, coke production, and so on require energy inputs even though the resulting output of these activities yields an intermediate energy demand. Explicit modeling of these energy conversion processes is restricted to the generation of electrical energy because of the variety of fuels used to produce the product. In the EDAS, electrical energy requirements for final demand are satisfied by conventional fossil fuel generation, hydroelectric generation (hereafter, *hydro*), and/or nuclear generation. Since hydro and nuclear generation, which are exogenous, are typically baseload, they are subtracted from total demand requirements to give the necessary amount to be supplied by conventional fossil fuels. Behavioral equations then suggest the total energy demand and the combination of coal, oil, and natural gas needed. The demand for these three energy types by electric utilities is then added to final energy primary energy demand.

No attempt is made to independently reflect the inroads that emerging energy technologies will make in satisfying aggregate energy demand. The Carter administration's *Domestic Policy Review of Solar Energy*,[1] for example, hoped that by the year 2000 some 20 percent of energy demand would be met by renewable resources. As demonstrated repeatedly, the attainment of such a goal is not realistic.[2] Because of the uncertainties inherent in the development of renewables, a delineation of the potential impacts were subjectively developed based on a consensus of the estimates of researchers in the area. The resultant values were then, as with hydro and nuclear generation, subtracted from electrical energy generation, since most of the penetration of emerging energy technologies will result in the direct displacement of that energy type. This is not entirely correct and hence will slightly bias the forecasts. But since the consensus forecasts suggest that renewables will contribute less than 0.05 percent, the overall effect will be minimal.

THE EQUATION SPECIFICATIONS

It is not necessary to recount in excrutiating detail the exact form of all of the components of the EDAS. Many of the elements are given in the preceding chapters. As noted earlier, because of data availability two of the sector energy demands were estimated at the regional level (the residential sector and the electric utility sector), one was estimated by pooling the component parts (the industrial sector), and the last was estimated solely on the basis of national aggregate data (the transportation sector). As a result the forecasts will be national aggregates.

It is useful to quickly review the nature of the equations for each sector and close any of the remaining specification gaps. The discussion is ordered in a fashion similar to that given in Table VI.1.

The residential sector energy demand component consists of four equations. The aggregate energy demand equation suggests that the quantity of all energy consumed in the sector is a function of economic activity, weather, a distributed lag on real energy prices, and qualitative regional differences. The expenditure shares for oil, natural gas, and electrical energy are a function of each of the energy prices. These latter three equations together with knowledge of the price of each energy type will indicate how aggregate energy demand (from the first equation) is allocated among energy types.

Aggregate energy demand in the industrial sector, computed as the demand for one of the factors of production, is a linear-in-logarithms function of technological change, output of manufactured goods, and the relative price of output to the price of energy. Four equations determine the mix of energy types by two-digit Standard Industrial Classification (SIC). Cost shares for coal, oil (both distillate fuel oil and residual fuel oil), natural gas, and electrical energy are functions of the price of each of the energy types. Observe that no attempt is made to correct for thermal efficiencies.

The energy demand in the transportation sector focuses on

four different subsectors and interfuel substitution. Explicit account is taken of motor gasoline demand, diesel fuel demand, aviation (jet) fuel demand, and electric rail demand. Because of data limitations, water transportation is not overtly modeled. Motor gasoline demand is based on a simultaneous determination of the stock of automobiles and the utilization of that stock. The automobile stock is a function of economic activity and a generalized price (which, in turn, is a function of the price of motor gasoline, the sticker price of cars, vehicle miles traveled, automobile efficiency, and a discount rate). Utilization, or vehicle miles traveled, is a function of the price of motor gasoline, economic activity, weather, and the rate of unemployment. Lagged effects of changes in the price of motor gasoline and the price of automobiles is reflected in the computation of the generalized price. The diesel fuel demand by trucks, buses, and—to a limited extent—automobiles is a function of the level of industrial economic activity and a distributed lag on diesel fuel price. Aviation fuel demand is a simple function of per capita income, the price of jet fuel, and a time trend to reflect the increase in the desirability of air travel. The demand for electrical energy by the transportation sector, reflecting electric rail travel, is hypothesized to be a function of disposable income and the price of electrical energy.

Expenditure shares on each of the types of energy consumed by the subsectors of the transportation sector—namely, motor gasoline, diesel fuel, aviation fuel, and electrical energy—is modeled by hypothesizing that the relative expenditure on each energy type is a function of the price of all of the energy types. The suggestion is that this will effectively capture intermodal shifts in response to changing relative prices.

The conversion of the electrical energy generation requirements into primary energy inputs (coal, oil, and natural gas) is modeled in two stages. The first specifies the demand for energy by the sector to be a function of the price of electrical energy relative to an aggregate energy price, technological change, as well as total generation. No provision has heretofore been made to forecast the generation requirements. To do so requires an approach similar to that used elsewhere.[3]

Total demand plus a factor for transmission losses, i.e., generation, Q, is a function of economic activity (per capita disposable income), Y, the number of customers, C, weather (heating degree days, HDD, and cooling degree days, CDD), and the price of electrical energy, P_{ee}; here the subscript t denotes a time trend. Since the specification is for the long run, no lagged values are incorporated. The precise specification for generation is thus

$$\log Q_t = \beta_0 + \beta_1 \log Y_t + \beta_2 \log C_t + \beta_3 \log HDD_t \quad (6.1)$$
$$+ \beta_4 \log CDD_t + \beta_5 \log P_{ee} + \beta_{6_t},$$

where log denotes logarithm to the base e, and $\beta_0, \beta_1, \ldots, \beta_6$ are parameters to be estimated.

The parameter estimates were obtained by pooling regional data over the period 1961–1978. The generation data, number of customers data, and electrical energy price data (average price) were obtained from the Edison Electric Institute.[4] The economic activity data and weather data came from the U.S. Department of Commerce.

One would expect the coefficient on price to be negative, indicating that an increase in price will result in a reduction in the quantity demanded and hence generation. The coefficients on economic activity and the number of customers should be positive, as should the coefficients on the weather variables.

Observe that in the specification no provision is made for the substitution of other energy sources in response to relative price changes. Thihs is handled in the other sectoral components.

Serial correlation appears frequently when one uses multiple time series with trend components. This proved to be the case here so the Cochrane–Orcutt technique was used to correct for it.[5] The estimation technique used is the iterative seemingly unrelated regression method first developed by Zellner.[6]

The equation previously discussed was fit to regional time series data covering 1961–1978. The estimation results are given in Table VI.1. Values in parentheses are the standard errors of the estimates. The values present an interesting picture of the response of generation (i.e., demand) to changing exogenous factors. Consumers, in the aggregate, are responding to changing electrical energy prices. The estimates suggest

Table VI.1. Generation of Electrical Energy

Parameter	Estimate[1]
β_0	−5.2610
	(2.3395)
β_1	0.9621
	(0.4409)
β_2	0.0625
	(0.0174)
β_3	0.0591
	(0.0255)
β_4	0.0379
	(0.0121)
β_5	−0.6211
	(0.3031)
β_6	0.0097
	(0.0041)
ρ^2	0.2234
	(0.0947)
$\bar{R}^2$	0.9863
D.W.[3]	2.01

Notes:
[1] Standard errors of estimates in parentheses.
[2] Serial correlation coefficient.
[3] Durbin-Watson statistic.

that for each 1 percent rise in energy prices, generation falls by 0.62 percent. This is clearly within the −0.05 to −1.0 range obtained by others.[7] The effect on generation of changes in the level of economic activity is similarly important, with the results indicating that for each 1 percent rise in per capita disposable income, generation increases by 0.96 percent. The remainder of the included endogenous variables are likewise significant.

With an objective forecast of generation, one is able to relate output to fuel input requirements. To get fossil fuel demand by electric utilities, hydro and nuclear generation must be netted out. To do so, requires forecasts of hydro and nuclear generation. This is accomplished by extrapolating past trends—subject to planned additions to capacity. Expenditure shares of each of the fossil fuels used in the generation process are estimated as functions of all of the fuel prices, with the expenditure mix reflecting changes in relative fuel prices.

Electrical energy generation losses are important and modeled as a fixed proportion technology. Historically, transmission losses have been approximately 8 percent of total generation.[8] This is the factor employed.

As an addendum, refinery losses must be accounted for. Historically, they have averaged 6 percent for the United States.[9] Consequently, the demand for energy by SIC 29 must be inflated appropriately.

This completes the discussion of the equation specifications. Final comments are needed on a couple of points. First, conversion activities other than that of electrical energy are not modeled. Coal and natural gas consumption in the energy sector are totally subsumed in the consumption of these fuels in other sectors. Second, the common energy accounting unit is the British thermal unit (Btu).[10] Thus, the results of the simulations from the EDAS is measured in these units.[11]

SOME REFLECTIVE CAVEATS

Uncertainty

In any forecasting and simulation system there are inherent uncertainties. These uncertainties can be grouped into three primary categories: (1) the assumptions concerning the behavior of the exogenous variables may not be realized; (2) the analysis may not adequately reflect the nature of energy demand; and (3) the data on which the EDAS is calibrated might be inaccurate.

The assumptions used in making the forecasts will be based partly on a variety of possible future federal government actions and partly on policies currently in force and legislation already in place. Moreover, due to the uncertainty associated with the price on imported crude oil, several possibilities must be entertained.

The EDAS has been structured in such a fashion as to be consistent with contemporary neoclassical microeconomic theory. To the extent that this theory concerning the way consumers respond to various factors is amiss, or if the functional forms have been incorrectly selected yielding a misleading demand structure, then inaccuracies in the forecasts will result.

Data errors are also sources of uncertainty in the forecasts. Some care has been taken in specifying the origin of the time series. Most of the data come from federal agencies charged with accurately measuring the series. There are some limitations in the data, however. Thus, for example, use of the energy data from the Annual Survey of Manufacturers (ASM) when calibrating the industrial demand model presents a shortcoming, namely, the existence of captive energy in three of the component industries. (Captive energy is energy consumption that does not pass through the market and hence is not reflected in the ASM data. This will have the effect of understating actual energy consumption.) Thus, coal which is used to make coke, a large item in the production of steel, is not picked up as a purchased fuel. Likewise, for petroleum refining, residual fuel oil, still gas, distillate fuel oil, and petroleum coke—all are captive. Finally, in the pulping industry there is a large and growing component of captive energy. Overall, these omissions are not significant and hence little concern is warranted.

Simplifying Assumptions[12]

To make the complexities of the real world conformable to a modeling structure, a number of simplifying assumptions must be introduced. These include exclusion, aggregation, range, symmetry, and fine lag. They are discussed in turn.

The concept of exclusion refers to the fact that any factor not explicitly included in the system is assumed to be unimportant in affecting the conclusions. Thus, in EDAS the attempt was to measure the input of a vector of variables on one or more elements. The nature of this input is then used to explain the economic process as well as forecast the future evolution of the variables of interest. The possibility of too restrictive simplifying assumptions arises when the vector of explanatory variables omits obviously important elements. Thus, when we were measuring the demand for electrical energy in a foregoing section, the omission of price, for example, as one of the explanatory factors clearly was not justified.

Problems of aggregation arise, as noted in Chapter I, when data on various subprocesses are combined, or aggregated, as if they were just a single process in order to reduce the number of elements dealt with to manageable proportions or because their number is too expansive. Thus, the structure of the residential component of the EDAS relied on a fairly high level of aggregation. Certain limitations, as noted, made this mandatory.

The data used in estimating the structural relationships of the simulation system came from observations made within the range of prior experience. If there is no structural change (i.e., change in the underlying way in which consumers respond to the various factors), then such data are acceptable in making projections outside the range of prior experience. If the data are used to make inferences outside of this range and the structure has changed, the credibility of the forecasts deteriorate. In each instance (for each of the forecasting components) as a result of this concern, the stability of the critical interfuel substitution response was examined. Fortunately, the results indicate the extent of interfuel substitution responses have remained unaltered (in a statistical sense).

The concept of symmetry refers to equal responses in both directions. Thus, for example, if the elasticities used to make forecasts are estimated over a historical period when reduced prices are accompanied by increased consumption, then under the symmetry assumption it is presumed that forecasts can also be made using these elasticities for periods when increased prices result in a decrease in the quantity demanded.

The length of time it takes for a given variable to completely respond to an exogenous stimulus is difficult to measure. An effort has been made to reflect the nature and extent of this distributed lag response, but in some instances the data are inadequate to measure how fast and effective the response will be.

CONCLUSIONS

The use of formal modeling systems of forecast the future has captivated out attention over the past 30 years. These systems serve the useful purpose of providing an explicit and organized framework and thus help to clarify the assumptions. They also promote communication between the model builder and users, as well as aiding in the accumulation of knowledge and making forecasts under altered assumptions. Moreover, structural models aid in discovering apparent inconsistencies and hence provide for a better understanding of the issues.

One of the shortcomings of the use of explicit modeling systems, however, is that the aura surrounding them often leads us to expect more than is justified. The forecasts derived from any energy model, including the one developed here, are subject to some imprecision. The estimation of parameters that are required to produce forecasts often necessitates assumptions that cannot be completely substantiated or simplifications that may obfuscate the representation of the system being studied. Moreover, radical changes and trend reversals in certain areas may well mean that assumptions employed currently, though valid prior to the variations, may no longer obtain. The absence of experience with the new structure can contribute to the impreciseness of the results.

A modeling system can be useful in organizing the information base and guiding decisions as well. Caution must be exercised however. If present conditions deviate significantly from the historical experience, it is possible that models will misdirect attention away from the appropriate concerns. (The focus on the energy consumption–GNP relationship is just one example of this.)

To recapitulate: Any model can be useful in the formulation of energy policy. It provides a framework to make intelligent choices. It facilitates the evaluations of the influences of the various elements that impact the decision. But a model is not reality. With that, we turn to the forecasts.

NOTES AND REFERENCES

1. Office of the President, *Domestic Policy Review of Solar Energy*. Washington, D.C.: U.S. Government Printing Office, 1978.

2. See, e.g., *The Market Penetration of Solar Energy*, Golden, Colo.: Solar Energy. Research Institute, 1979.

3. N.D. Uri, "The Demand for Electric Energy in the United States." *Energy Systems and Policy* 2:233–243, 1978.

4. Edison Electric Institute, *Statistical Year Book*. New York: Edison Electric Institute, annual.

5. D. Cochrane and G.H. Orcutt, "Applications of Least Squares Regression to Relationships Containing Autocorrelated Error Terms." *Journal of the American Statistical Association* 44:31–62, 1949.

6. A. Zellner, "An Efficient Method of Estimating Seemingly Unrelated Regressions and Tests for Aggregation Bias." *Journal of the American Statistical Association* 57:348–368, 1962.

7. L.D. Taylor, "The Demand for Electricity." *The Bell Journal of Economics and Management Science* 6:74–110, 1975.

8. Federal Power Commission, *The 1970 National Power Survey*. Washington, D.C.: U.S. Government Printing Office, 1971.

9. J.M. Blair, *The Control of Oil*. New York: Random House, 1976.

10. Technically defined, a Btu is the quantity of heat required to raise the temperature of 1 pound of water 1 degree Fahrenheit.

11. See S.S. Penner and L. Icerman, *Energy*, Reading, Mass.: Addison-Wesley Publishing Company, 1974, for more on measuring energy consumption.

12. These comments are similar to those of R. Stobaugh and D. Yergin, *Energy Future*. New York: Ballantine Books, 1979.

Chapter VII

Forecasting the Demand for Energy

INTRODUCTION

The principal use of the Energy Demand Analysis System (EDAS) is to examine the effects of various policies and exogenous factors on U.S. aggregate energy consumption/demand. (Note: demand and consumption are used synonymously.) Before launching into simulations with the EDAS, it is useful first to see how well it performs over the historical period and second to discuss the assumptions relevant for the exogenous variables.

PERFORMANCE

The oil pricing assumptions to be used are importantly dependent on oil consumption in the United States (as well as the rest of the world). Also, conservation policies to separate energy and economic growth focus on aggregate U.S. energy consumption. In view of these issues, consideration is warranted of the historical forecast performance of the EDAS over a period long enough to assess the system's capability to reflect longer-run trends in energy consumption. In principal a 15- or 20-year historical period is ideal since, by design, the system is intended for long-run simulation exercises. Consequently, the simulation exercise covers the period 1965–1980 (the latest period for which data are available). Actual values of the exogenous variables are employed in testing the system's adequacy. Note that the sample periods for the data observations are quite variable in length. The period 1964–1978 is a period of commonality. The final 2 years of comparisons are true forecasts in the sense that the models employed were not calibrated over them. They are not true forecasts in the sense that actual values of the exogenous variables were used in place of forecast values.

There are several measures of forecast accuracy. Short of discussing these (Granger and Newbold[1] provide a splendid exposition), it will simply be observed that a very common one—the mean absolute percentage error—is employed. Table VII.1 presents the forecast error for each year over the 1965–1980 period. The actual primary energy consumption data by type were taken from Volume 2 of the *Annual Report to Congress* of the U.S. Department of Energy.[2] Note that the 1980 data are preliminary. Overall, the EDAS performs remarkably well.

The first column of Table VII.1 indicates that the forecast error ranges from a low of 0.4 percent to a high of 8.2 percent. On average the forecasting accuracy is slightly better in the early part of the period. This is as we would expect given the growth in primary energy consumption over the horizon. In 1965 primary energy consumption was 50.91 quadrillion Btu's (hereafter *quads*), and by 1980 it had climbed to 70.36 quads. In 1980, the model is only off by 3.4 percent (2.3 quads) in predicting 1980 consumption. The implication is that the EDAS captures the long-term characteristics in a totally acceptble fashion. In the short-run the system does not perform quite as well, with errors in forecasting as high as 8.2 percent occurring.

The efficacy of capturing the secular evolution in energy consumption does not imply anything about movements in specific fuels over time. The mean absolute percentage errors for oil and natural gas suggest that this is a more challenging task, given that the percentage errors for each of these exceed that for aggregate energy. The particularly poor forecast years for oil and natural gas are associated with some supply anomaly. In the case of oil, the realized reduction in consumption in 1974 is not fully reflected in the model simulation. It appears

Table VII.1. Forecasting Errors[1] for United States Energy
Demand, 1965–1980

Year	Total Primary Energy	Primary Coal Demand	Primary Oil Demand	Primary Natural Gas Demand
1965	4.2	5.1	3.6	4.7
1966	5.0	5.2	4.8	5.1
1967	3.1	4.0	3.3	3.0
1968	2.5	2.3	2.9	2.1
1969	2.7	2.6	3.0	2.6
1970	0.4	0.1	0.7	0.3
1971	2.1	2.3	1.6	2.4
1972	3.6	3.7	3.5	3.9
1973	4.9	3.3	4.8	5.2
1974	8.2	7.5	11.5	8.1
1975	5.0	3.8	6.2	11.6
1976	3.9	2.5	4.4	6.9
1977	2.4	2.0	3.5	2.6
1978	1.9	0.6	2.4	3.7
1979	5.7	4.7	5.8	3.1
1980	3.4	2.7	5.6	4.1
Average[2]	3.7	3.3	4.2	4.3

Notes:
[1] Mean Absolute Percentage Error $= |\hat{Z}_t - Z_t|/Z_t * 100$, where Z_t is the actual value and $\hat{Z}_t$ is the forecast value.
[2] Average over the entire simulation horizon.

that nonquantifiable factors (e.g., non–price-induced conservation) were more important than the factors explicitly included. That is, for example, the forecast error is probably not due to improper measurement of the price elasticities since the consumption response to similar price movements in 1979 are satisfactorily captured. Similarly, the natural gas curtailments in 1975 and 1976 lead to an expanded forecasting error. A large number of qualitative elements were impacting demand in the heating season for those 2 years. These few exceptions aside, it appears that relative fuel prices do affect fuel choice decisions and these decisions are being reflected in the EDAS.

The errors of 5 to 11 percent for specific fuels translate into forecast errors of 2 to 4 quads. Given errors of this magnitude, for the short run a simpler procedure might perform better.[3] But the focus here is on the longer term, and such simple structural systems have been shown not to capture long-run trends.[4]

ASSUMPTIONS

The macroeconomic assumptions concerning the exogenous variables are taken from the *Energy Review*[5] of Data Resources, Incorporated. Without giving exhausting detail concerning the forecasts, it is useful to relate their essential ingredients. Real gross national product (GNP) is expected to grow 2.9 percent annually through 1990 and then decline to a 2.2 percent annual growth for the next decade. This latter decline is attributed to a reduction in the rate of growth of potential output. Disposable income moves coincidentally with the GNP trend. Industrial production is predicted to grow at 3.97 percent per annum for the period 1980 through 1990 and then fall to 3.0 percent per year during the 1990s. This lower rate of growth does not represent a slowdown in production but rather a normalization following the broken pattern of the 1970s.

Population will have an important effect on the overall growth of the economy due to its relationship to potential output. The growth rate of population is expected to average 1 percent annually during the 1980s and 0.7 percent during the 1990s. This slowing of growth during the last decade of the century will hamper the ability of the U.S. economy to reach growth rates of 3 percent or even the 2.5 percent considered normal during the 1960s and 1970s.

The rate of unemployment is forecast to improve steadily from a peak of 7.9 percent in 1980 to 5.9 percent in 2000. This reflects increased investment and the reuse of currently underutilized capacity as the economy straightens out following the period of stagnation in the late 1970s.

Sales of automobiles (reflecting changes in the stock of automobiles) are forecast to average 3.3 percent growth from 1980 to 1990 and reach a peak of 9.4 million (just above the 1978 level) in 1988. During the 1990s they are expected to decline at a rate of 1 percent per year, a victim of demographic movements and energy costs. New car efficiences are based on the rising real cost of motor gasoline.

It is assumed that as prices rise demand for fuel-efficient cars will increase and manufacturers will continue to produce increasingly efficient cars each year. The average efficiency of new automobiles is calculated as a function of the real price of motor gasoline 2 years prior and a technical weighted efficiency index (miles per gallon per pound of vehicle weight). This calculated efficiency is forecast to rise from 20.1 MPG (miles per gallon) in 1980 to 28.9 MPG in 2000.

Weather, to the extent it can be forecast, is expected to be normal.

Energy price assumptions are heavily dependent on the supply profile. As a result of petroleum decontrol, all domestic oil categories will reach the expected world oil price by 1982, with slight variations due to quality differentials. The real price of imported crude (in 1980 dollars) is anticipated to rise at 3.4 percent per year from 1980 to 1990 and at 3.2 percent per year from 1990 to 2000. In view of the current soft tone of the world crude market, the marginal price of imported oil is set equal to the average price of imported oil over the forecast horizon.

The average coal price is based on a weighted average of the regional long-run marginal coal prices from the coal model of Data Resources, Incorporated, and the inflation adjusted average contract price of the previous period. The Coal Model Simulation assumes a 10 percent return on equity, enforcement of the state implementation plans for air emissions by 1985, and federal severance taxes of 15 cents per ton on deep-mined coal and 35 cents per ton on strip-mined coal. The real price of coal is, therefore, forecast to rise at 3.8 percent per year through 1990 and 2.2 thereafter.

Electrical energy prices are very sensitive to assumptions regarding (1) generating plant capacities, (2) plant costs, and (3) the allowable rate of return on invested capital. Additions and retirements for plants are taken from various utility surveys. Likewise, the utility capital costs are gleaned from industry sources. The return on invested capital in the electric utility sector is a weighted averge of the return on common and preferred stock, long-term debt, and public financing. These rates of return are all average rates of return and are forecast using the current rate of return rolled in with the average return, as new capital expenditures are made. Given these assumptions, the forecast for electrical energy prices is for a 4 percent increase per year for the 1980–1990 period and 1.3 percent between 1990 and 2000.

Two critical suppositions influence natural gas pricing. First, the years for phaseout of price controls have been reduced in anticipation of the current administration's announced policy changes. Second, the long-term pricing path of natural gas is expected to be more competitive with residual fuel oil than with the more costly distillate fuel oil. The ceiling price of natural gas is assumed to follow the Natural Gas Policy Act of 1978 (NGPA) through 1982; beginning in 1983, however, it is allowed to to increase at a faster rate toward eventual decontrol in 1987. Previously, the phaseout period was to occur between 1985 and 1990. Actual forecast price movements translate into a 7.3 percent annual rise between 1980 and 1990 and a 4.1 percent yearly rise for the last decade of the twentieth century.

ORIENTATION

Attention in the past few years has been directed at energy demand and supply relationships for the remainder of the twentieth century. The forecasts by the Ford Foundation[6] have been followed by studies such as those done by the Organization for Economic Cooperation and Development (OECD),[7] Data Resources, Incorporated,[8] the U.S. Department of Energy,[9] Stobaugh and Yergin,[10] the Office of Technology Assessment,[11] and the Workshop on Alternative Energy Strategies (WAES).[12]

In evaluating what is being done here, it is useful to compare our results with those of one of the aforementioned studies. Since the WAES study is among the better known, it is selected for comparison. The WAES report is especially important since it forecasts a shortage of crude oil for the United States under a varying set of assumptions.

Against a policy background, the WAES results are especially pessimistic, indicating that the response of energy demand to price variations is insufficient to reach energy self-sufficiency by stimulating production and/or inducing conservation (recall the discussion in Chapter I). As an example, WAES argues that for a variety of reasons the price mechanism is insufficient to produce and allocate energy efficiently and effectively. Assuming that the members of the Workshop were not economists and that their concept of efficiency is different than that employed by the economics profession, the reasons for the nonattainment of the desired objectives have to do with the magnitude of the price changes needed to bring about the desired goals.

While the WAES report's principal hypothesis is that there is a critical problem as to the long-run supply of oil at prevailing prices, is the correctness of this sufficient to permit us to conclude that demand response (even through the artificial manipulation of energy prices via, for example, a tax) is too small to handle a shortage?

The results of the WAES report have relevance to these questions as they pertain to energy conservation. The EDAS provides a mechanism through which the impact of economic growth and energy prices on energy demand can be evaluated. Through simulations, the effect of an energy tax on energy consumption, for example, can be quantified. Rather than relegating price responsiveness to actions by the Organization of Petroleum Exporting Countries (OPEC) and government tax initiatives to the nonexistent category, such responses are an empirical question and must be examined as such. Moreover, slower economic growth resulting from, among other things, lower population and productivity growth may also lessen the difference between realized oil consumption and domestic production. Does this simply that the problem will continue without any lessened severity?

It is useful, before simulating with the EDAS, to reiterate its constraints. It is a demand-side structure describing the quantity of energy demanded as a function of exogenously determined energy prices and a set of macroeconomic variables. No attempt is made to reflect production responses to price changes. The EDAS will produce for a given vector of energy prices and other exogenous variables the quantities that will be demanded. There is no presumption that these quantities will be precisely forthcoming.

The next section outlines the scenarios on which the model simulations are based. The subsequent section presents the energy consumption profiles to the year 2000 resulting from these assumptions. The final section of the chapter examines the responses in the various sectors to determiine whether some energy-using sectors offer greater promise for conservation than others.

SCENARIO DISCUSSION

This section delineates the scenarios selected to examine the evolution of energy demand over the period 1980–2000. The scenarios are selected to demonstrate the response of the demand for energy to changes in energy prices and economic activity. The magnitude of the changes to these exogenous variables is chosen with an eye on their plausibility.

Scenario 1: Base Case. The Base Case scenario utilizes the assumptions previously discussed in the section on assumptions. Recall that some of the variables of interest were dependent on the nominal values of pecuniary variables. Consequently, a forecast of the rate of inflation is required. After the price of oil, this is undoubtedly the most difficult forecasting requirement. For our purposes, inflation will be measured by movements in the GNP deflator. Recall that in the EDAS it is changes in relative prices of energy types that induce substitution responses. Since energy prices are tied to the inflation rate, the actual rate of inflation in the substitution context is not important. Inflation, however, is critical in the setting of aggregate sectoral energy demand. As before for many of our assumptions, we use the forecast rate of inflation provided by Data Resources, Incorporated. The average value for the 1980–1990 period is 9.5 percent while the average for the 1990–2000 period is 6.4 percent.

Two other exogenous factors that have heretofore not been discussed are forecasts of the rate increase in hydroelectric and nuclear generation. In these instances, the Data Resources, Incorporated, forecasts are used. The hydroelectric generation forecasts, representing the reduction in available sites, are 1.4 percent increase for 1980–1990 and 0.0 percent for 1990–2000. Nuclear generation forecasts, assuming no moratorium on new capacity, are for increases of 9.1 percent and 3.9 percent for the 1980–1990 decade and 1990–2000 decade, respectively.

Scenario 2: Slow Economic Growth. The economic recovery following the disastrous impact of the Arab oil embargo in late 1973 and early 1974 has not yet been fully accomplished. Since then the rate of growth in economic activity has been significantly below historical trends and the rate of growth in labor productivity has been almost nonexistent.[13] This has led many forecasters to assume that the growth in labor productivity and hence economic activity will be below past trends.[14] Consequently, the Slow Economic Growth scenario presumes a 0.9 percent slower growth in GNP and the corresponding measures of economic activity (e.g., per capita disposable income). Likewise, industrial production increases at a 0.9 percent slower rate. All other assumptions remain unchanged from the Base Case scenario.

As a caveat, there are a large number of reasons for the observed decline in labor productivity during the decade of the 1970s. The growth of productivity in the U.S. economy was rapid by historical standards. In the last half of the decade of the 1960s, however, the rate began to mitigate. This slackening was not particularly problematic from the long-term growth perspective until 1974. It was partly the result of stochastic fluctuations in determinants of output that typically display irregular movements—primarily a reduction in the intensity of use of employed labor and capital from the peak reached in 1965–1966. The remainder was the consequence of developments that were inevitable. These included transfer of surplus workers from farming to nonfarm jobs in which the workers produce output of greater value. This diminished as the pool of such labor was depleted. The proportion of inexperienced workers among the employed was expanded by significant increases in the working population that was under 25 years old, a rising relative proportion of employed to population in the young age groups, and entry of more women into the labor force. Further, the costs of government regulations (that ostensibly had benefits in excess of costs) began to impact upon productivity. These factors do not provide particularly good insights into the productivity slowdown in more recent years. Beginning in 1974, the decline in productivity became increasingly severe and the factors responsible for the fall prior to 1974 were no longer sufficient to explain the observed decline. Most productivity series—e.g., output per person employed, output per hour, and output per unit of input—show essentially the same pattern.

No consensus has emerged as to the important determinants of the decline in productivity. Many diverse suggestions have been forthcoming. Among the factors suggested as being contributory are curtailment of expenditures on research and development, increased lag in the application of knowledge due to the aging of capital, regulation and taxation, impairment of efficiency by inflation, lessening of competitive pressure, changes in the quality of management, and rising energy prices. While no single hypothesis seems to provide a probable explanation of the sharp change in productivity after 1973, the one that has generated the most controversy is the rise in energy prices. We have before us a complete spectrum of opinions. At one extreme, Rasche and Tatom[15] attribute the entire decline in productivity to the rise in energy prices. At the other extreme, Denison[16] finds only 0.1 percent of the decline (i.e., a statistically insignificant amount) attributable to energy prices.

The sharp reduction in the growth of productivity coincided with the sudden rise in OPEC oil prices in late 1973 and early 1974. We can identify three effects of the oil price increase. First, the rise in the imported oil price resulted in a deterioration in the terms of trade that reduced the ability of the U.S. to produce goods and services by approximately 1 percent. This, however, did not directly change productivity.[17] Consequently, this factor can be relegated to the background. Next, in an effort to reduce current and future imports, the government intervened with controls over fuel consumption and fuel choice. Finally, the rise in the price of energy relative to the other factors of production resulted in a substitution of capital, labor, and materials for energy. Given this, what was the effect on output per unit of input?

The effect on output per unit of input of a given percentage decline in energy use depends on the elasticity of substitution between energy and capital. If the elasticity of substitution is 1 (Berndt and Wood[18] suggest that this is approximately correct, whereas we obtain a value of 0.6 in Chapter III), and if energy constitutes approximately 5 percent of total input into the production process (Schurr and Darmstadter[19] find this to be the right order of magnitude), then a 1 percent fall in energy consumption without a corresponding change in capital would result in a net reduction in output as well as in output per unit by 0.05 percent (or 0.03 percent, if the results of Chapter III are accepted).

There is one caveat regarding these estimates. The amount by which the rise in energy prices after 1973 affects productivity is difficult to calculate precisely since it is impossible to delineate exactly what would have happened to total energy consumption because the pre-1974 experience was not uniform. The energy/output ratio has declined historically since, say, 1947, but this decline has not been homogeneous, i.e., it has not been unvarying in its rate of reduction. To infer what happened in the post-1973 era based upon prior experience is at best a rough approximation.

Scenario 3: Rising World Crude Oil Prices. Any energy assessment is set amid the high uncertainty characterizing the world oil market. In 1979, the tight world oil market and the uncertainty resulting from the Iranian revolution caused world oil prices to soar. At the beginning of 1979, the weighted average official price of internationally traded oil was $13.77 per barrel. By January 1, 1980, the price was $26.55, a 93 percent increase. New York spot market prices for motor gasoline, which stood at $21.42 per barrel in January 1979, were as high as $50.82 in December 1979.[20] But as stocks grew, spot prices subsided.

In 1980, production in Iran continued to fall from 3 million barrels per day in December 1979 to 1.4 million barrels per day by September 1980. By the fourth quarter of 1980, the Iran–Iraq war reduced Iranian production below 1 million barrels per day. Oil exports from Iran and Iraq dropped near to zero shortly after hostilities broke out, but some oil was reported flowing from the region during the fourth quarter of 1980.[21] A supply disruption of the order of magnitude discussed here would increase world oil prices $6 to $12 per barrel, depending on demand pressures for OPEC oil.[22] The Iran–Iraq war may affect world oil prices and supplies much less adversely than did the Iranian revolution, however. Before the war's outbreak, oil stocks in the industrial countries were at relatively high levels and oil demand was depressed. Moreover, Saudi Arabia led efforts to temporarily increase oil production to insulate the world oil market from potential negative effects. The impact on world oil markets, however, could become more serious if this war (or another) intensifies or if it spreads to other producers in the Middle East.

The foregoing is meant only to highlight the extreme uncertainty associated with forecasting world crude oil prices (and hence domestic prices since under the Reagan administration's decontrol program they will soon become coincident). Given this, it is assumed that crude oil prices will rise at a yearly rate of 5 percent for the remainder of the century.

This scenario will capture the extent of interfuel substitution relative to the Base Case. A test for significant interfuel substitution against oil products can be performed. There is good reason to believe that the price of petroleum products will rise relative to the prices of other conventional fuels as it did during the 1970s.

GENERAL FORECAST RESULTS

Base Case

One can become inundated with an extraordinarily large quantity of numbers in model simulations. To mitigate such an eventuality, only average growth rates are reported, the intent being to give a flavor of the evolution of demand. Little is lost by foregoing exhaustive detail, given the overall objectives of providing insights into the nature of the impact of energy on the economy and the extent of interfuel substitution.

Table VII.2 summarizes the aggregate results for the three scenarios simulated over the period 1980–2000. The table reports total primary energy consumption and the consumption

Table VII.2. Summary of Forecasts (in Percent)

Scenario	1980 to 1990	1990 to 2000
1. Base Case		
Primary Energy	1.7	1.9
Primary Coal	5.4	4.6
Primary Oil	−0.4	0.1
Primary Natural Gas	−0.5	−0.2
2. Slow Economic Growth		
Primary Energy	1.1	1.2
Primary Coal	5.0	4.1
Primary Oil	−1.1	−0.5
Primary Natural Gas	−0.8	−0.5
3. Rising World Crude Oil Price		
Primary Energy	1.6	1.8
Primary Coal	6.4	5.7
Primary Oil	−1.6	−1.3
Primary Natural Gas	0.0	0.3

of primary coal, oil, and natural gas. The Base Case scenario indicates that the growth in aggregate energy demand will fall well below the 3.4 percent growth rate of the period 1950–1980. Several factors explain the average 1.8 percent growth rate. First, the Arab oil embargo of 1973–1974 and the Iranian crisis in 1979 resulted in sharply higher energy prices. These price increases yield reduced energy consumption. After the lagged price effects have had their entire impact, the growth rate increases in the mid-1980s but still results in a rate of growth below the historical rate. There are a couple of reasons for this. The lower rate of population growth yields a smaller growth rate in the labor force and hence a reduced rate of economic growth. By examining the Slow Economic Growth scenario of an average 1.15 percent growth in energy consumption versus the 1.8 percent growth rate in the Base Case scenario, it is observed that slower economic growth of 0.9 percent accounts for a reduction in aggregate energy demand growth by 0.65 percent. Additionally, unlike the historical pattern where energy prices fell relative to the price of other goods and services, the Base Case scenario has the price of energy increasing relative to other goods and services prices. In the aggregte, future energy consumption growth rates are expected to fall below historical growth rates due to a combination of slower economic activity, high energy prices, and demographic factors.

How do the results here compare to those obtained by others? The Ford Foundation[23] obtains a forecast of energy growth for the remainder of the century of 1.7 percent, very close to the results given here; it assumes a GNP growth rate of 3.3 percent, slightly above what is assumed here. The estimates from the EDAS suggest a large response to changes in the level of economic activity, and hence an almost identical forecast results. A Shell Oil Company publication,[24] on the other hand, forecasts almost no change in energy consumption; Shell's assumption concerning economic growth puts the figure at 2.7 percent. Finally, Data Resources, Incorporated, predict a 1.3 percent growth in aggregate demand based upon slightly less optimistic economic growth assumptions than employed here.[25]

The growth paths for individual fuels are significantly different. From Table VII.2, coal growth is projected at an average of 5 percent per year, well above the 1.7 percent average for all energy. Alternatively, the growth rates of oil and natural gas are, on average, actually negative. The increased growth of coal over the forecast horizon is attributable to the expected relative fuel price changes. All fuel prices are expected to rise, but oil and natural gas experience a relatively more rapid increase than coal. Substantial interfuel substitution is occurring.

The growth of coal use at a relatively faster pace than growth in oil or natural gas demand is attributable to another factor. As discussed previously, different energy types serve as principal fuels in the various sectors (see below), growing at differential rates. Thus, on average the primary fuel consumption will grow at different rates even though no appreciable interfuel substitution is occurring within a given sector. This is being reflected in these forecasts.

Once again it is useful to compare the results presented here with those obtained by others. Shell forecasts oil demand to fall by 2.5 percent per year, natural gas to rise by 0.5 percent, and coal to increase slightly by 2.1 percent a year. Data Resources, Incorporated, on the other hand, forecasts oil consumption to fall by 0.4 percent and natural gas consumption to decline by 0.3 percent. Coal consumption is expected to rise by 3.9 percent. These latter results are not very different from those obtained with the EDAS.

Slow Economic Growth

An assessment of the Slow Economic Growth (SEG) scenario relative to the Base Case scenario provides some interesting insights about the relationship between economic growth and energy consumption. The SEG scenario, based upon a 0.9 percent economic activity growth rate below the Base Case scenario, indicates a growth in primary energy consumption of 1.15 percent as compared to the 1.8 percent average of the Base Case. One can conclude that energy demand and economic activity, other things being equal, are intertwined. Energy consumption and economic growth are not simply stochastic processes that have a high correlation coefficient.

The conclusion that primary energy consumption declines 0.7 percent for each 1 percent fall in GNP is consistent with some of the sectoral results that finds the income elasticity of energy demand in the neighborhood of 1. The SEG scenario yields a significant (although not proportional) reduction in the growth rates of individual fuels. Relative to the Base Case scenario, the consumption of coal falls from 5.4 to 5.0 percent per year. The decline in the growth rate for both oil and natural gas are intensified.

Even though the magnitudes of reduction in the growth rates of the various fuels vary, the strong relationship that exists between aggregate primary energy consumption and economic activity carries over to the individual fuels. The conclusion: a principal ingredient affecting fuel consumption is economic growth.

Rising World Crude Oil Price

If there should be another event or sequence of events leading to yet another precipitous rise in the price of crude oil and hence the prices of all refined petroleum products, we will witness a slight reduction in overall energy demand but more significantly a quite sizeable decline in primary oil consumption. This scenario emphasizes the considerable possibilities for long-run interfuel substitution. Relative to the Base Case, coal consumption rises significantly and so does natural gas consumption. The oil consumption growth rate declines from -0.4 to -1.6 percent. The implied own-price elasticity is -0.76, while the oil/natural gas cross-price elasticity is 0.38 and the oil/coal cross-price elasticity is 0.62. Clearly, coal is the preferred fuel in the aggregate if and when the price of oil rises faster than expected.

SECTOR ENERGY DEMAND

It is useful to examine the impact upon sectoral demand for energy that the aforementioned scenarios are expected to have. To accomplish this, they are discussed sequentially.

Residential Sector

Table VII.3 portrays the response of the residential sector under the various scenarios. A reduction of 0.9 percent per

Table VII.3. Summary of Residential Forecasts (in Percent)

Scenario	1980 to 1990	1990 to 2000
1. Box Case		
Total Energy	0.6	1.2
Oil	-2.4	-1.8
Natural Gas	1.5	1.2
Electrical Energy	3.2	2.7
2. Slow Economic Growth		
Total Energy	-0.4	0.2
Oil	-3.4	-2.8
Natural Gas	0.5	0.2
Electrical Energy	2.2	1.7
3. Rising World Crude Oil Price		
Total Energy	0.3	0.8
Oil	-3.8	-3.4
Natural Gas	2.5	2.3
Electrical Energy	4.0	3.8

year in the growth of real per capita income leads to a decline in the energy growth rate from an average of 0.9 to an average of −0.1 over the 20-year period. Energy consumption is not only very responsive to the level of economic activity, it is also quite responsive to energy price variations. The Rising World Crude Oil Price (RWCOP) scenario indicates a deceleration in energy consumption growth from an average 0.9 percent to an average 0.55 percent.

There is a considerable amount of variation in the growth rates between energy types. In the Base Case, electrical energy grows more rapidly than either natural gas or oil (which, in fact, is expected to fall). This simply represents a continuation of the trend established in the past two decades. The RWCOP scenario suggests that both natural gas and electrical energy are equally substitutable for oil.

The results suggest that in the residential sector there is considerable potential for energy conservation of both energy in general and oil in particular. The decrease in the rate of growth of energy consumption from 0.9 to 0.55 percent when we compare the RWCOP scenario to the Base Case scenario attests to this potential. For oil, the indication is that an average 1.7 percent increase in the price of crude oil and hence refined petroleum products relative to the other energy types yields a reduction in the growth rate of oil consumption from −2.1 to −3.6 percent per year. Such conservation occurs primarily in space cooling and cooking.

Industrial Sector

The growth in aggregate energy demand in the industrial sector closely emulates the growth rate in all sectors. Table VII.4 reports that the Base Case scenario shows an average 1.85 percent growth rate. Aggregate energy consumption is affected by both the level of economic activity and energy prices. With a fall in industrial output of 0.9 percent, the demand for energy as a factor of production falls by 1 percent, from 1.85 percent to 0.85 percent. This result follows from the output elasticity of 1.2 estimated previously. Not surprisingly, the impact of slow growth on the consumption of specific energy types are proportionately distributed. The growth rates

Table VII.4. Summary of Industrial Forecasts (in Percent)

Scenario	1980 to 1990	1990 to 2000
1. Base Case		
Total Energy	1.9	1.8
Coal	4.9	3.5
Oil	−1.4	−1.7
Natural Gas	−0.1	−2.3
Electrical Energy	2.4	2.2
2. Slow Economic Growth		
Total Energy	0.9	0.8
Coal	3.9	2.5
Oil	−2.4	−2.7
Natural Gas	−1.1	−3.3
Electrical Energy	1.4	3.2
3. Rising World Crude Oil Price		
Total Energy	1.6	1.6
Coal	5.2	3.8
Oil	−1.8	−2.3
Natural Gas	0.0	−2.2
Electrical Energy	3.0	2.9

for coal, oil, natural gas, and electrical energy decline by approximately 1 percent.

The impact of energy prices on aggregate energy consumption is of interest. The RWCOP scenario suggests that energy consumption will decline from 1.85 to 1.6 percent, reflecting the previous finding that energy is substitutable for capital.

Significant interfuel substitution effects can be observed in the industrial sector. In the Base Case scenario, energy type growth rates are appreciably different between fuels. The growth rates for both oil and natural gas are considerably less than the rates for coal and electrical energy.

The RWCOP scenario clearly demonstrates that coal and electrical energy are the primary energy substitutes for oil. Compared to the Base Case, the growth rate of coal increases from an average 4.2 to 4.5 percent, while the growth rate for electrical energy accelerates from 2.3 to 2.95 percent. By way of contrast, the growth rate of natural gas is little affected.

The results bear a significant policy implication, namely, that in the industrial sector there is considerable potential for price-induced energy conservation both for total energy consumption as well as for oil.

Transportation Sector

Relative to aggregate energy consumption, the rate of growth in demand for energy in the transportation sector is expected to be less, averaging 0.3 percent through the year 2000 (see Table VII.5). The lower-than-the-aggregate average growth rate is attributable primarily to the influence of motor gasoline consumption. The importance of economic activity can be observed from the SEG scenario, where motore gasoline consumption falls by 0.65 percent given a 0.9 percent fall in the level of economic activity.

Another factor contributing to the relatively lower growth is the response to the high motor gasoline price increases oc-

Table VII.5. Summary of Transportation Forecasts (in Percent)

Scenario	1980 to 1990	1990 to 2000
1. Base Case		
Total Energy	−0.1	0.7
Motor Gasoline	−2.5	−0.9
Diesel Fuel	5.8	3.2
Aviation Fuel	2.9	2.4
Electrical Energy	4.3	5.1
2. Slow Economic Growth		
Total Energy	−0.7	0.0
Motor Gasoline	−3.2	−1.6
Diesel Fuel	5.0	4.4
Aviation Fuel	1.6	0.8
Electrical Energy	3.5	4.3
3. Rising World Crude Oil Price		
Total Energy	−0.5	0.4
Motor Gasoline	−3.1	−1.4
Diesel Fuel	5.4	2.8
Aviation Fuel	2.5	2.0
Electrical Energy	4.2	5.0

curring during the decade of the 1970s (due to the price rises engineered by OPEC) as well as the planned decontrol of the price of oil. As can be seen from the RWCOP scenario, motor gasoline consumption falls by 0.6 percent given a rise in price of 1.7 percent.

There is an obvious policy implication from these results. A tax on motor gasoline that raises the price is an effective method of curtailing the consumption of refined petroleum products. On reflecting upon this it should be realized, given the nature of the price response previously assessed, that the impact of any such tax will be spread out over a number of years. It takes time for consumers to adapt the utilization and automobile stock to the disincentive offered by the higher price.

Electric Utility Sector

As indicated in Table VII.6, the total consumption of fossil fuels by electric utilities will grow at a somewhat higher rate than aggregate energy consumption in the economy. This is

Table VII.6. Summary of Electric Utility Forecasts
(in Percent)

Scenario	1980 to 1990	1990 to 2000
1. Base Case		
Total Fossil Energy	3.4	3.2
Coal	4.2	4.4
Oil	−5.5	−6.5
Natural Gas	−3.0	−3.2
2. Slow Economic Growth		
Total Fossil Energy	2.5	2.3
Coal	3.4	3.5
Oil	−6.4	−7.4
Natural Gas	−3.9	−4.1
3. Rising World Crude Oil Price		
Total Fossil Energy	3.2	3.0
Coal	6.5	6.3
Oil	−7.0	−7.8
Natural Gas	−0.5	−0.7

simply a reflection of the above-average growth in the demand for electrical energy in the residential, industrial, and transportation sectors. Overall, electrical energy will claim an increasing portion of the future energy mix. Generation of electricity (and hence fuel consumption) is quite responsive to changes in the level of economic activity, as suggested in the SEG.

The Base Case scenario reveals a different growth rate for the various fuels. Coal consumption is expected to contribute the strong upward trend established in the 1970s, while oil and natural gas will continue on a downward course. The difference in the projected profile, in large part, is the result of the relatively large increases in oil and natural gas prices.

In the generation of electrical energy, interfuel substitution is at work. Comparing the RWCOP scenario with the Base Case scenario, we see that oil price increases which are 1.7 percent faster give a more rapid decline in oil consumption with a coincident rise in coal consumption and a less rapid fall in natural gas consumption. The oil consumption decline occurs in part due to the reduction in demand for electrical energy whose price, due to the rising world crude oil price, has increased. The remainder is a consequence of substitution.

CONCLUSIONS

The possibility of an increasing price of world crude oil and the uncertainty surrounding the level of economic activity are the significant factors influencing the forecast of primary energy demand in the United States. The rising price of crude oil reduces petroleum product consumption absolutely as well as inducing some substitution between fuels. A fall in the level economic activity yields a net reduction in energy demand.

The impact of an increasing relative price of oil is not uniform across sectors. In the industrial sector, for example, where energy decisions are fairly sensitive to cost factors, there is a distinct shift away from oil to alternative fuels, particularly coal. For example, builders of new industrial boilers—which can produce steam using either coal, oil, or natural gas—have a marked incentive to select coal. In the electric utility sector, existing oil-fired generating units can be retired as quickly as noneconomic factors (e.g., the approval of public utility commissions) permit. In the transportation sector, which is heavily dependent upon petroleum products, motor gasoline actually declines because of the use of more efficient vehicles and reduced travel by automobile.

NOTES AND REFERENCES

1. C.W.J. Granger and P. Newbold, *Forecasting Economic Time Series.* New York: Academic Press, 1977.
2. U.S. Department of Energy, *Annual Report to Congress,* Volume 2. Washington, D.C.: U.S. Government Printing Office, 1981.
3. For example, the approach suggested by G.E.P. Box and G. Jenkins, *Time Series Analysis.* San Francisco: Holden-Day, Inc., 1971.
4. N.D. Uri, "A Mixed-Time Series-Econometric Approach to Forecasting Peak System Load." *Journal of Econometrics 9*(January):155–171, 1979.
5. Data Resources, Incorporated, *Energy Review,* Spring 1981. Lexington, Mass.: Data Resources, Incorporated, 1981.
6. Ford Foundation, *A Time to Choose.* Cambridge, Mass.: Ballinger Publishing Company, 1972.
7. Organization for Economic Cooperation and Development, *Energy Prospects to 1985—An Assessment of Long Term Energy Developments and Related Policies.* Paris: Organization for Economic Cooperation and Development, 1974.
8. Data Resources, Incorporated, *Energy Review.* Lexington, Mass.: Data Resources Incorporated, semiannual.
9. U.S. Department of Energy, *Annual Report to Congress.* Washington, D.C.: U.S. Government Printing Office, 1980.
10. R. Stobaugh and D. Yergin, *Energy Future.* New York: Ballantine Books, 1980.
11. Office of Technology Assessment, *World Petroleum Availability, 1980–2000.* Congress of the United States, Washington, 1980.
12. Workshop on Alternative Energy Strategies, *Energy: Global Prospects 1985–2000.* New York: McGraw-Hill Book Company, 1977.
13. N.D. Uri and S.A. Hassanein, "Energy Price, Labor Productivity, and Causality," processed, 1981.
14. See, e.g., Department of Energy, *Annual Report to Congress,* Volume 3. Washington, D.C.: U.S. Government Printing Office, 1981.
15. R. Rasche and J. Tatom, "Energy Resources and Potential GNP." *Federal Reserve Bank of St. Louis Review 59:*10–24, 1977.
16. E. Denison, "Explanations of Declining Productivity Growth." *Survey of Current Business 59:*259–268, 1979.
17. E. Denison, *Accounting for Slower Growth.* Washington, D.C.: The Brookings Institution, 1979.
18. E.O. Berndt and D.O. Wood, "Technology, Prices and The Derived Demand for Energy." *The Review of Economics and Statistics 56:*259–268, 1975.

19. S. Schurr and J. Darmstadter, *Nuclear Power Issues and Choices*. Cambridge, Mass.: Ballinger Publishing Company, 1977.
20. Department of Energy, *Weekly Petroleum Status Report*. Washington, D.C.: U.S. Government Printing Office, weekly.
21. Department of Energy, *International Energy Industries*. Washington, D.C.: U.S. Government Printing Office, September 1980.
22. Department of Energy, *Annual Report to Congress*. Washington, D.C.: U.S. Government Printing Office, 1981.
23. Ford Foundation, *A Time to Choose*. Cambridge, Mass.: Ballinger Publishing Company, 1972.
24. Shell Oil Company, *Energy Outlook*. New York: Shell Oil Company, 1980.
25. Data Resources, Incorporated, *Energy Review*, Autumn 1980. Lexington, Mass.: Data Resources Incorporated, 1980.

Chapter VIII

Conclusion

INTRODUCTION

The preceding empirical estimation and scenarios yield some policy inferences that are relevant to the controversy between the energy conservationists and those emphasizing energy supply as alluded to in Chapter I. It is useful to enumerate these points in this final chapter. Before doing so, however, a few reflections are in order.

This study set out to look at the demand for energy in the United States by using a consistent, unified approach. One must not rely on a single forecast of energy demand, however. Concentrating on only one aggregate view of the future neglects unavoidable uncertainty. Energy markets are too complex, energy products are too diverse, and the unknowns are too many to be reduced confidently to a single description far ahead in time. The growth of the economy, policies designed specifically to affect demand, the resolution of important environmental debates, and the movement of energy prices will all have significant impacts on the level and composition of future energy demand. The inherent uncertainties associated with these issues are large and can never ex ante be fully resolved. But the type of analysis found in the foregoing pages can help to understand the implications of the uncertainties and to define the range of future demand levels as well as the likely response to changes in important conditions.

The events in 1973 and 1979, with dramatic changes in the world oil market, stimulated considerable interest in the options available for changing the growth in energy consumption. The examination here suggests that there are substantial opportunities to substitute capital as well as change consumption patterns in order to reduce the consumption of energy.

In view of the opportunities for reducing energy consumption, it is not essential to produce a single, exact forecast based on only one view of the future. The long-run economic impact of higher energy prices may be much smaller than might be anticipated for energy. If the effect of higher energy prices and reduced energy consumption is to substitute other factors in place of unavailable energy supplies rather than to curtail otherwise productive endeavors, then the economic cost of higher energy can be relatively small. The decisions today do not depend critically on the evolution of demand within the most likely range. There is no intention, however, to imply that no cost is associated with making wrong decisions or that individual economic agents are not confronted with difficult choices. Instead, the foregoing analysis suggests that broad policy recommendations for action today do not change if demand grows as suggested herein, assuming that advantage is taken of the opportunities to adapt as more information is obtained.

The adjustment process that will be required as advantage is taken of the proposed long-term substitutions is another matter. In the short run, the U.S. economy is less flexible, i.e., our ability to alter the mix of energy demand is limited. In the immediate term, the demand for energy is determined essentially by the existing stock of energy-using appliances and equipment, which can be modified (turned over) only slowly. The process of change, as the energy system is remodeled, will have impacts on all sectors of the economy.

The problem confronting the United States, then, is to manage the adjustments. The costs and benefits of energy use must be accurately assessed, and the best way to do this from the economic perspective is to make usre that all energy consumers have adequate and reliable information. This can be accomplished mainly through the price mechanism, which reflects the relative scarcity of energy so that alternative energy uses may be compared.

If price accurately reflects the scarcity of energy—including the effects of resource exhaustion, the environment, national security, and so forth—and if the consumers pay these prices, then the aggregate level of energy demand, in an efficiency sense, will be correct. It is most important that the system operate in such a fashion as to give the correct signals to the consumer. The projection of the Base Case demands was the starting point for our analysis of the energy system. If there is some difficulty in meeting these demands and this difficulty is translated into higher energy prices, the capability to change the uses of energy will lead to a reduction in demand until the costs of further energy consumption just balances the benefits.

This is what the theory of price tells us.[1] In past periods the market mechanism worked well, and it will work in the future if allowed. The higher prices of energy do not constitute a crisis, nor are they the essence of the energy problem. If the adjustment to a new era of relative energy scarcity can be managed, hhigher energy prices will be the solution. A reasonable energy pricing policy will initiate the necessary adjustments that must be made by providing the requisite incentives to make the needed substitutions. With higher energy prices, future energy demands as demonstrated will be below the historical trend—a trend that was established during a period of relative decreasing energy prices.[2]

Given these reflections, the conclusions of the foregoing analysis are summarized in the next section.

GENERAL CONCLUSIONS

The general conclusions are enumerated as follows:

1. In the short run as well as in the long run, there is a significant relationship between energy consumption and economic growth. The estimation results for each of the sectors, when reflecting short-term effects, suggest somewhat limited interfuel substitution in addition to the substitution of capital, labor, and materials for energy. In the long run, there is likewise a close interrelationship. The Base Case scenario when compared to the Slow Economic Growth (SEG) scenario high-

lights the importance of energy as an input into the industrial production process as well as its role in the residential sector (households). Energy growth moves coincident with economic growth. To the extent that rising energy prices keep pace with increases in the level of economic activity, then energy growth will be slightly below but highly correlated with economic growth.

2. Over the long term, price induced conservation is viable. The Rising World Crude Oil Price (RWCOP) scenario showed that higher crude oil prices can lead to reductions in the rate of growth of energy consumption. De facto, it is possible to change the energy/GNP ratio and energy inputs into the production process through price-induced energy conservation and the attendant interfuel substitution. The length of time required to achieve these adjustments is equal to the period of capital stock turnover. Energy conservation is realized through the price mechanism. It should be observed, however, that there are costs (both implicit and explicit) to conservation.

3. Conservation policies, to the extent they are adopted, should be comprehensive and not limited to a specific sector. There has been a tendency to focus conservation efforts on the industrial and transportation sectors while leaving the residential sector and electric utilities unattended. This is not justified in light of the results which suggest that energy conservation is achievable in all sectors. In fact, the residential sector is more responsive to price incentives than the industrial sector.

4. If the primary area of concern is with national security, U.S. conservation policies would do well to concentrate on crude oil and refined petroleum product consumption. If the supposition that energy supplies are virtually unlimited in the foreseeable future at higher prices is accepted, then the main concern rests in the national security implications of dependence on foreign crude oil. A comparison of the Base Case scenario and the RWCOP scenario demonstrates that a rising oil price will lead to interfuel substitution and a corresponding fall in the consumption of oil. While there is no intention to imply that the national security issue is the same as the energy problem, there is a strong hint that more selectivity is needed in identifying those fuels for which conservation is appropriate.

5. An objective balance between conservation policies and incentives to stimulate production is essential. There is no effort in the foregoing analysis to assess the potential for expanded energy production. It is latently assumed, however, that there is a considerable potential for such expansion. Like energy conservation, expanded producton can make a contribution to improving the energy future of the United States. If both conservation and expanded production are possible only within certain bounds, then policies must be balanced to take advantage of both sides of the market.[3]

CONSUMMATORY REMARKS

There is considerable flexibility as to how energy is used for various activities. In the past, it has not been particularly important how much energy was consumed for any given objective. There was little reason to be concerned with this issue. It was cheaper to leave windows broken (in a production setting) than to replace them. The situation, however, has changed. It is no longer economically optimal to ignore the potential for increasing the efficiency with which energy is used.

Energy conservation is not so simple to achieve as it might at first appear. It is diffuse and has no clear, identifiable constituency in the fashion that coal, for example, does. Public policy must create the environment for proper exploitation. For conservation to have the kind of impact it should have, there must be a skillful combination of signals including price incentives, public information, and possibly regulation. Only in this way can conservation become as economically attractive to individual economic agents as it is to society as a whole.

The U.S. economic system has repeatedly demonstrated a responsiveness to incentives; however, in the energy area, public policy has been remiss. Until now there has been an inability to evaluate the true prices and risks of conventional alternatives. The consequence is an inability to assess the relative costs of incentives that will promote conservation.

The basic ingredients of a meaningful conservation policy are straightforward.[4] First, the price system must give a clear and consistent signal concerning energy. Prices must reflect replacement costs. Second, incentives should provide conservation measures with a fair chance to substitute for high-cost imported crude oil. Finally, adequate information must be accessible to all consumers about the possibilities of energy conservation.

The United States can potentially consume less energy than it currently does through conservation. Only the future knows whether it will.

NOTES AND REFERENCES

1. See, e.g., G. Stigler, *The Theory of Price*. New York: Macmillan Publishing Company, 1947.

2. For more on this, see W.E. Hogan, "Dimensions of Energy Demand" in *Selected Studies on Energy*, H. Landsberg (ed.). Cambridge, Mass.: Ballinger Publishing Company, 1980.

3. See N.D. Uri, *Dimensions of Energy Economics*. Greenwich, Conn.: JAI Press Inc., 1981.

4. L.R. Stobaugh and D. Yergin, *Energy Future*, New York: Ballantine Books, 1979, offer an interesting discussion in this area.

Index

Aggregation problem, 11
Allen, R.G.D., 38, 51, 77, 91, 110, 121, 132, 145
Allen partial elasticities of substitution, 75, 108
Almon, S., 34, 50, 120
American Gas Association, 50
Annual Report to Congress, 14
Annual Survey of Manufactures, 79
Appliance stock utilization, 34
Arrow, K.J., 20
Arrow, K.J., H. Chenery, H. Minhas, and R. Solow, 90, 127, 145
Atkinson, S. and R. Halvorsen, 127, 145
Aviation fuel demand, 105

Bailey, E.E., 119
Barten, A.P., 40, 51, 78, 91, 111, 121, 134, 145
Barzel, Y., 145
Baughman, M., and P. Joskow 19, 50
Baumol, W.J., 120

Berndt, E., and L. Christensen, 24, 28, 62, 90, 144
Berndt, E., and C. Watkins, 51
Berndt, E., and D. Wood, 56, 89, 180
Blair, J., 158
Box, G.E.P., and G. Jenkins, 90
Box, G.E.P., and D. Pierce, 90
Branson, W.H., 89
Bridge, J.L., 27
Brookhaven Energy System Optimization Model, 21
Brown, R.L., J. Durbin and J. Evans, 47, 52, 87, 91, 117, 121, 141
Bureau of Mines, 50

Cato, D., M. Rodekohr and J. Sweeney, 96, 99–100, 119
Census regions, 40, 51
Chern, W.S., 51
Chow, G., 52, 91, 99, 117, 120, 121, 141, 146
Chow test, 47
Christensen, L.R., 23
Christensen, L.R., and W. Greene, 130, 145

Christensen, L.R., and D. Jor-
genson, 62, 90
Christensen, L.R., D.W. Jorgen-
son, and L.J. Lau, 28, 50,
90, 145
Christensen, L.R., and L.J. Lau,
120
Coal reserves, 4
Cochrane, D., and G. Orcutt, 99,
120, 152, 158
The Conference Board, 90
Constant elasticity of substitution,
70, 127
Cramer, J.S., 26

Darmstadter, J., 33, 50
Data filtering, 63
Deaton, A., and J. Muellbauer,
26
Degree day, 49
Denison, E., 180
Diesel fuel demand, 102
Diewert, W., 144
Directional causality, 58
Dynamic elements, 12

Edison Electric Institute, 50
Elasticity of Demand, 5
Elasticity of substitution, 77
Electrical energy generation,
151ff
Electrical energy price sensitivity,
163
Energy expenditures in the
United States, 23
Energy Demand Analysis System,
147
Energy Modeling Forum, 21, 28
Energy substitution, 4

Factors of production, 53
Factor substitutability, 56
Faruqui, A., 90

Faucett Associates, 63, 90
Federal Energy Administration,
27
Fisher, F.M., 11, 27
Ford Foundation, 180
Forecasting uncertainty, 154
Freeman, S.D., 3, 26
Fuss, M., and D. McFadden, 89

Galatin, M., 145
Gantzer, 28
Generalized price measure, 97
Goldfeld, S., and R. Quandt, 51,
91, 121, 146
Gollop, F., and S. Karlson, 146
Gould, J., and C. Ferguson, 90
Granger, C.W.J., 58, 90
Granger, C.W.J., and P. New-
bold, 160, 180
Green, D.L., and A.B. Rose, 119
Griffin, J., 46, 51, 84, 91, 96,
101, 120, 129, 145, 146
Grunfeld, Y., and Z. Griliches,
90

Halvorsen, R., 90, 91
Harper, D.V., 121
Haugh, L., 90
Henderson, J., and R. Quandt,
89, 145
Hick's neutral technological
change, 70
Hirst, E., and J. Carney, 27
Hitch, C.J., 26
Hoch, I., 29, 49
Houthakker, H.S., 10, 26, 27, 96
Houthakker, H.S., and L. Tay-
lor, 14, 19, 49, 102, 120
Houthakker, H.S., P. Verlager,
and D. Sheehan, 119
Hogan, W., 26, 188
Homogeneity, 37

Homogeneous energy aggregate, 24

Hudson, E.A., and D. Jorgenson 23, 28, 84, 91, 140, 146

Indirect translog utility function, 32

Interfuel substitution, 45, 53ff, 73ff, 107ff, 131ff

Jackson, J., 27
Johansen, L., 89
Jorgenson, D., 50
Jorgenson, D., and E. Berndt, 23, 28, 74, 75, 90, 127, 144

Keynes, J.N., 26
Kmenta, J. and R. Gilbert, 40, 51, 78, 91, 112, 121, 134, 144, 145
Kulssh, D.J., 120

Labor productivity, 167
Law of demand, 6
Leff, H.S., and R. Mack, 91
Leontieff-type production function, 69, 129
Linear homogeneity, 112, 127

Marginal product of energy, 70
Marshall, A., 5, 76
Maximum likelihood estimates, 40, 78
Mean absolute percentage error, 161
Measurement issues, 10
Mid-range energy forecasting system, 21
Milne, J.A., 99, 120
Medel stability, 86, 117, 141
Motor gasoline demand, 95ff

National petroleum product supply and demand, 15
Natural gas policy act, 164
Nelson, J.P., 50
Nerlove, M., 72, 90, 130, 145
Netschert, B., 26
Nissen, D., and D. Knapp, 46
Nordhaus, W.D., 26, 50
Norman, M.R., and R. Russell, 91

O'Brien, J., 120
Organization for Economic Cooperation and Development, 165
Organization of Petroleum Exporting Countries, 2

Partial elasticities of substitution, 38, 110, 132
Penner, S.S., and L. Icerman, 158
Phillips, A., 120
Pierce, D., and L. Haugh, 61, 90
Pindyck, R., 33, 49
Powerplant and industrial fuel use act, 85
Price, J.M., 90
Price possibility frontier, 75, 131
Production frontier, 74

Quandt test, 41, 79, 113, 135

Ramsey, J., 10, 27, 96, 120
Rasche, R., and J. Tatom, 180
Regional classification, 146
Regression stability, 47
Residential fuel mix, 30

Samuelson, P.A., 6, 26
Scherer, C.R., 130, 145
Schumpeter, J.A., 26

Schurr, S., and J. Darmstadter, 169, 181
Seitz, W., 145
Shephard's lemma, 38, 76, 131
Shephard, R., 50, 91, 120, 145
Short-term integrated forecasting system, 16–17
Sims, C., 90
Simultaneous equation bias, 10–11
Speculative effect, 13
Staley, J., 120
Standard industrial classification, 53
Standardized efficiency factor, 19
Stigler, G., 188
Stobaugh, R., and D. Yergin, 164, 180, 188
Stone, R., 9, 10, 27
Structural model stability, 47, 117, 141
Suits, D., 33, 50
Supernumerary income, 10
Sweeney, J., 120

Taylor, L.D., 10, 27, 46, 50, 119, 158

Thermal adjustment factor, 34
Time series analysis, 61
Translog price possibility frontier, 37, 108
Transportation demand for electrical energy, 106
Turvey, R., 140, 144, 146

Uri, N.D., 13, 27, 50, 89, 91, 144, 158, 180, 188
Uri, N.D., and S.A. Hassanein, 180
Uzawa, H., 38, 50, 77, 91, 120, 132, 145

Weather impact on energy consumption, 33
Wildhorn, S., 101, 120
Wold, H., and L. Jureen, 9, 27
Workshop on Alternative Energy Strategies, 164, 180

Zellner, A., 27, 40, 51, 78, 91, 111, 121, 133, 145, 152, 158